FOR ORGANS, PIANOS & ELECTRONIC KEYBOARDS

210

T0040952

'60s POP/ROCK

ISBN 978-0-7935-8241-9

7777 W. BLUEMOUND RD. P.O. BOX 13819 MILWAUKEE, WI 53213

E-Z PLAY ® TODAY Music Notation © 1975 by HAL LEONARD CORPORATION

E-Z PLAY and EASY ELECTRONIC KEYBOARD MUSIC are registered trademarks of HAL LEONARD CORPORATION.

Visit Hal Leonard Online at
www.halleonard.com

'60s POP/ROCK

CONTENTS

4	And When I Die	Blood, Sweat & Tears (1969)
10	Angel of the Morning	Merrilee Rush & The Turnabouts (1968)
13	Blue Velvet	Bobby Vinton (1963)
16	The Boy from New York City	The Ad Libs (1965)
20	Crying	Roy Orbison (1961)
23	Dancing in the Street	Martha & The Vandellas (1964)
26	Daydream Believer	The Monkees (1967)
32	Different Drum	The Stone Poneys featuring Linda Ronstadt (1968)
36	Do Wah Diddy Diddy	Manfred Mann (1964)
29	Do You Love Me	The Contours (1962)
40	Downtown	Petula Clark (1965)
42	Dream Baby	Roy Orbison (1962)
44	For Once in My Life	Stevie Wonder (1968)
46	Gentle on My Mind	Glen Campbell (1968)
50	Goin' Out of My Head	Little Anthony & The Imperials (1964)
56	Heatwave	Martha & The Vandellas (1963)
53	Hurt So Bad	Little Anthony & The Imperials (1966)
58	I Hear a Symphony	The Supremes (1965)
66	I Want to Hold Your Hand	The Beatles (1964)
63	I Will Follow Him	Little Peggy March (1963)
68	If I Were a Carpenter	Bobby Darin (1966)
70	Let's Hang On	The 4 Seasons (1965)
76	Let's Live for Today	The Grass Roots (1967)
82	Love Me Do	The Beatles (1964)

73	Love Potion Number 9	The Searchers (1965)
84	A Lover's Concerto	The Toys (1965)
86	Memories	Elvis Presley (1969)
88	Monday, Monday	The Mamas & The Papas (1966)
90	Money (That's What I Want)	The Kingsmen (1964)
92	My Girl	The Temptations (1965)
100	(You Make Me Feel Like) A Natural Woman	Aretha Franklin (1967)
95	Oh, Pretty Woman	Roy Orbison (1960)
104	On Broadway	The Drifters (1963)
106	Only the Lonely	Roy Orbison (1964)
108	Please Mr. Postman	The Marvelettes (1961)
112	Please Please Me	The Beatles (1964)
114	Reason to Believe	Rod Stewart (1971)
120	Return to Sender	Elvis Presley (1962)
117	Soul and Inspiration	The Righteous Brothers (1966)
122	Spinning Wheel	Blood, Sweat & Tears (1969)
125	Stop! In the Name of Love	The Supremes (1965)
130	Sugar, Sugar	The Archies (1969)
133	Suspicious Minds	Elvis Presley (1969)
136	True Grit	Glen Campbell (1969)
139	Twist and Shout	The Beatles (1964)
142	Viva Las Vegas	Elvis Presley (1964)
150	Wedding Bell Blues	The 5th Dimension (1969)
152	What Now My Love	Sonny & Cher (1966)
145	You Keep Me Hangin' On	The Supremes (1966)
154	You've Lost That Lovin' Feelin'	The Righteous Brothers (1965)
156	You've Made Me So Very Happy	Blood, Sweat & Tears (1969)
159	Registration Guide	

And When I Die

Registration 4
No Rhythm

Words and Music by
Laura Nyro

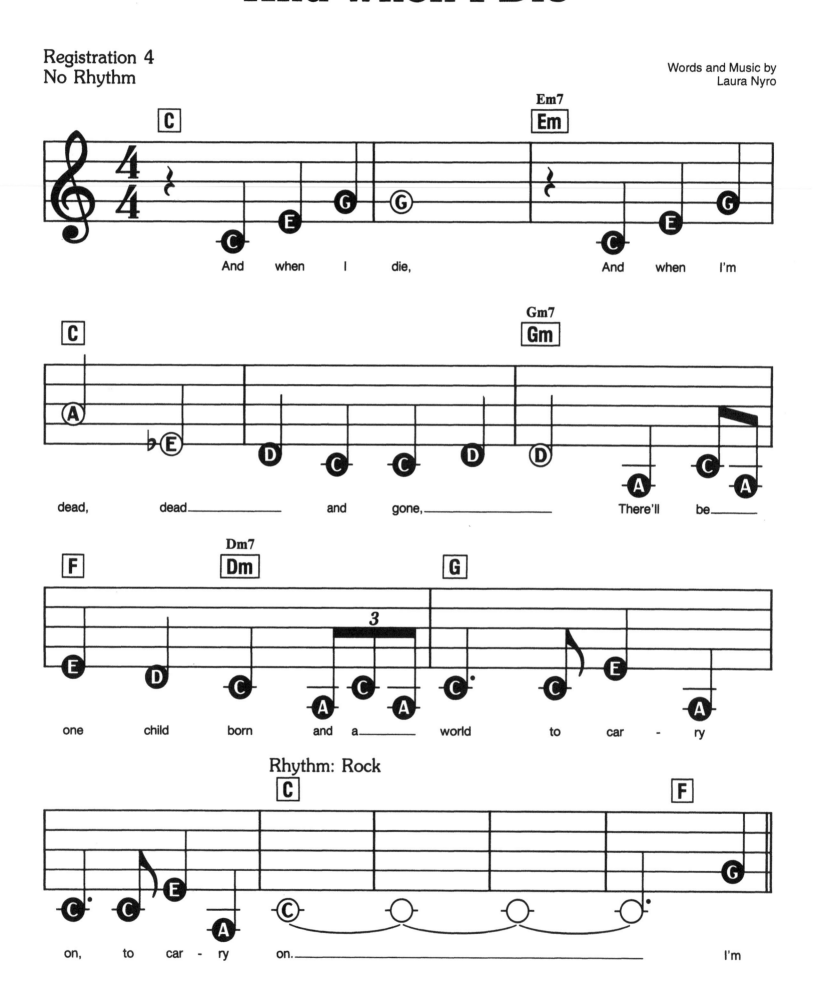

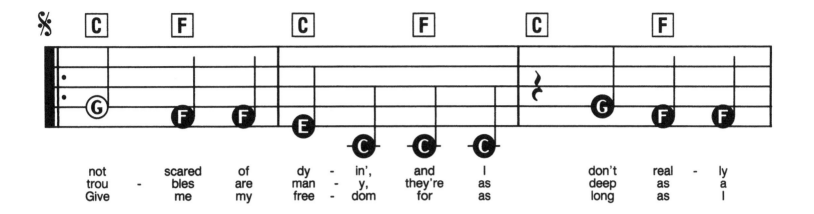

not scared of dy - in', and I don't real - ly
trou - bles are my man - y, they're as I as deep as a
Give me my free - dom for as long as I

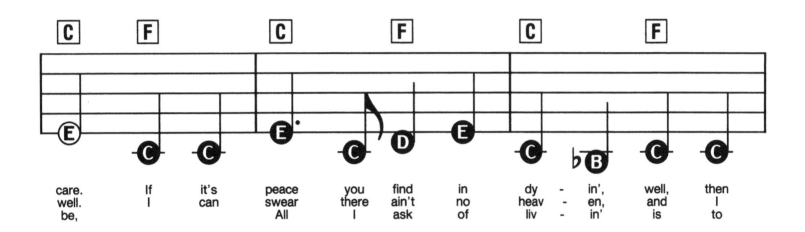

care. If it's peace you find in dy - in', well, then
well. I it can swear there ain't no heav - en, and I
be, All I ask of liv - in' is to

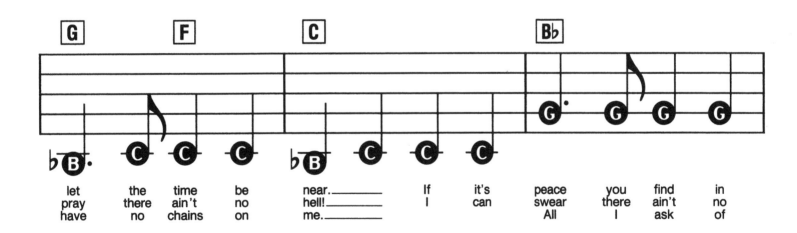

let the time be near. If it's peace you find in
pray there ain't no hell! I it can swear there ain't in no
have no chains on me. All I ask of

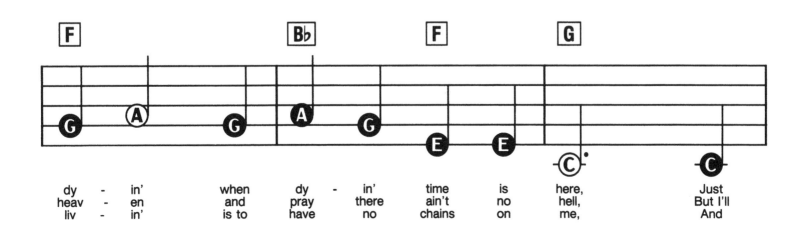

dy - in' when dy - in' time is here, Just
heav - en and is to pray have there no chains hell, But I'll
liv - in' is to me, And

6

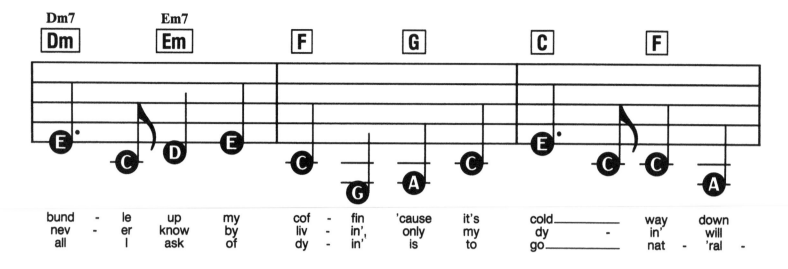

bund - le up my cof - fin 'cause it's cold_____ way down
nev - er know my by liv - in', only it's my dy_____ in' will
all I ask of dy - in' is to go_____ nat - 'ral -

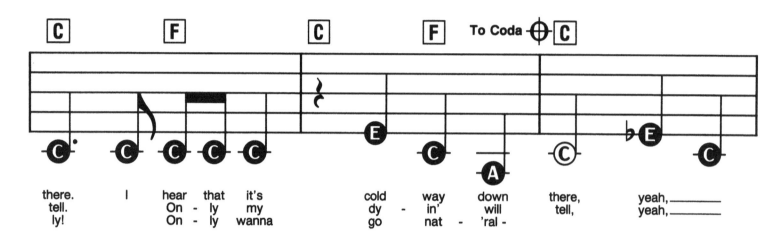

there. I hear that it's cold way down there, yeah,_____
tell. On - ly my dy - in' will tell, yeah,_____
ly! On - ly wanna go nat - 'ral -

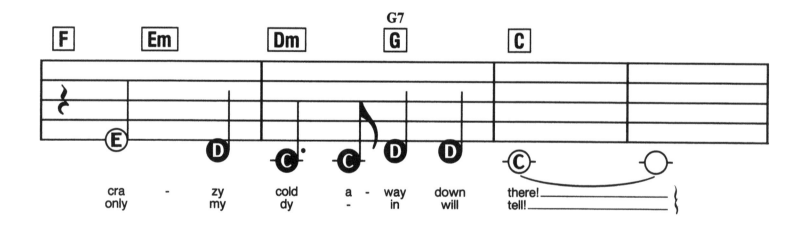

cra - zy cold a - way down there!_____
only my dy - in will tell!_____

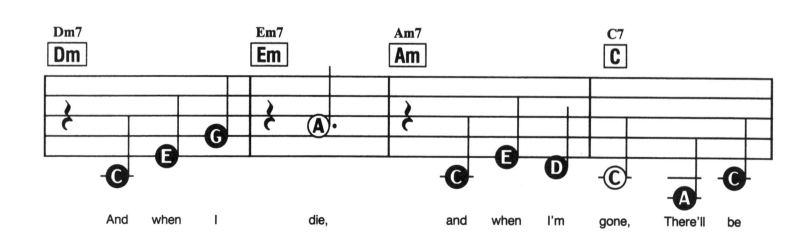

And when I die, and when I'm gone, There'll be

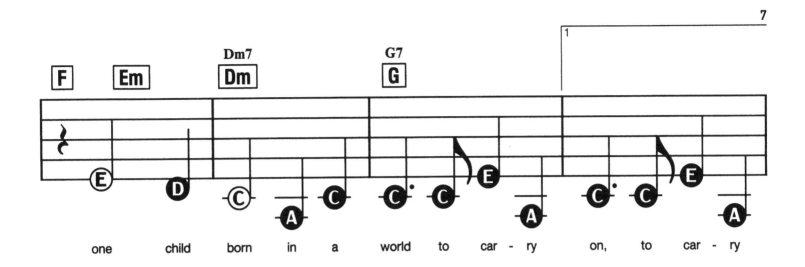

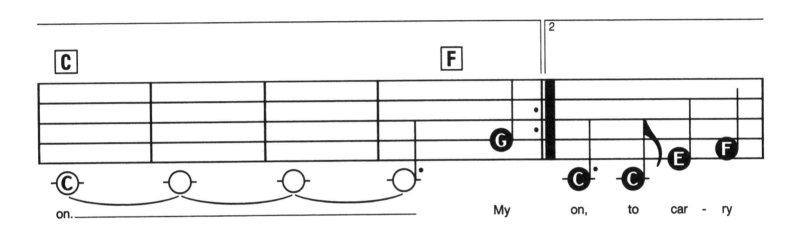

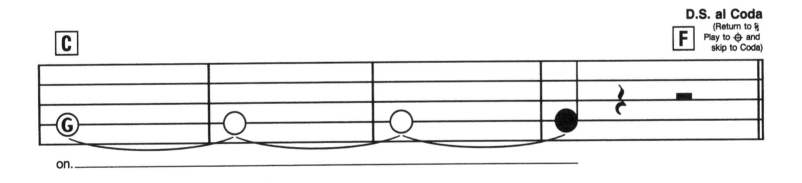

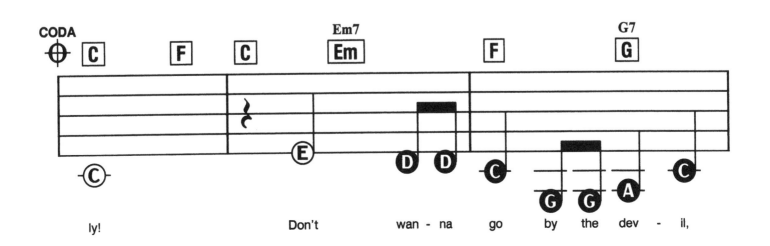

8

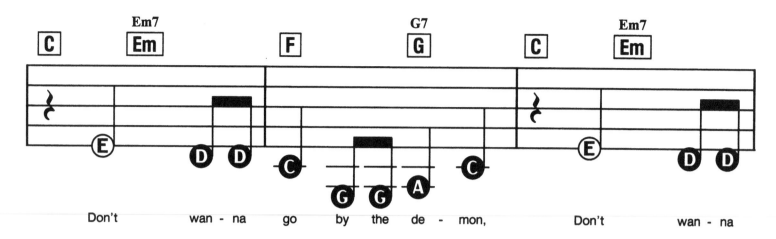

Don't wan - na go by the de - mon, Don't wan - na

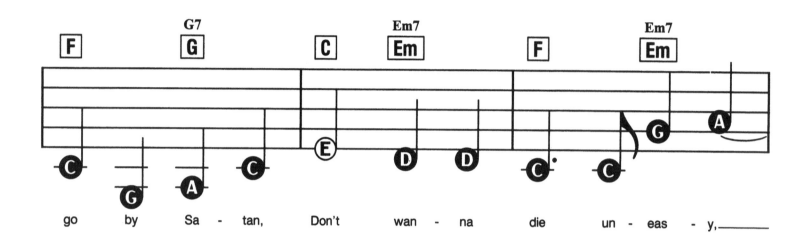

go by Sa - tan, Don't wan - na die un - eas - y,

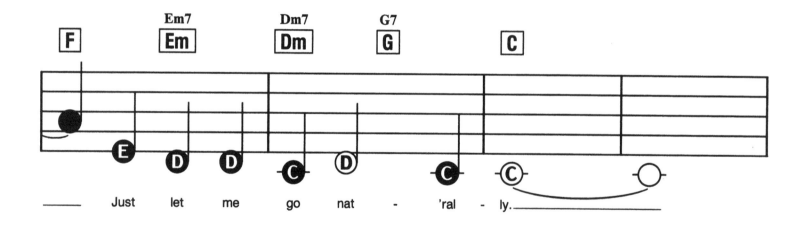

Just let me go nat - 'ral - ly.

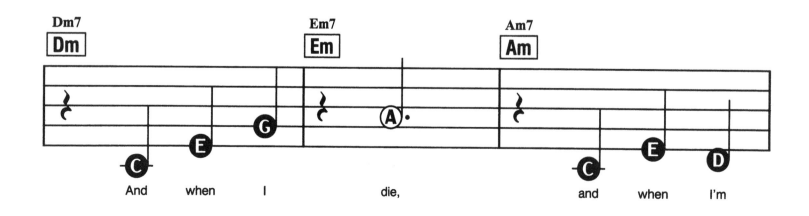

And when I die, and when I'm

9

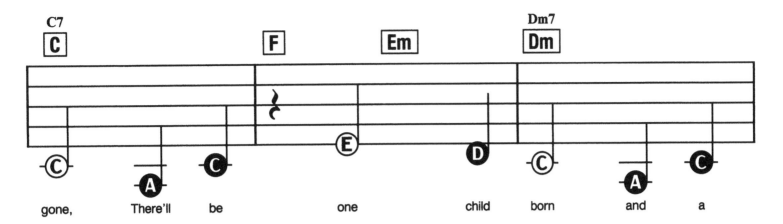

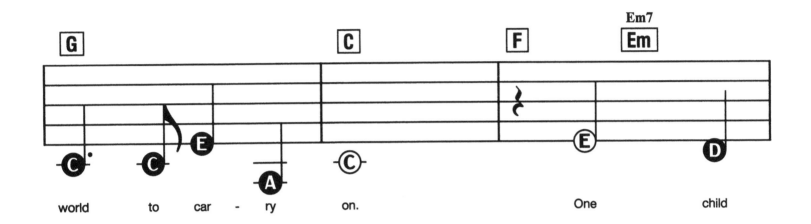

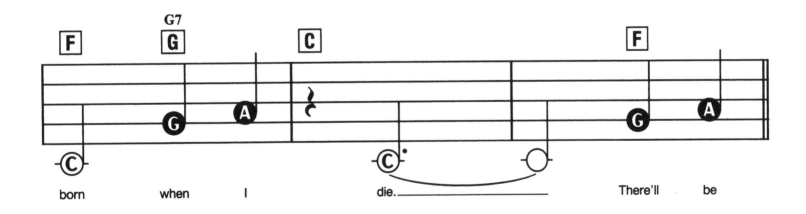

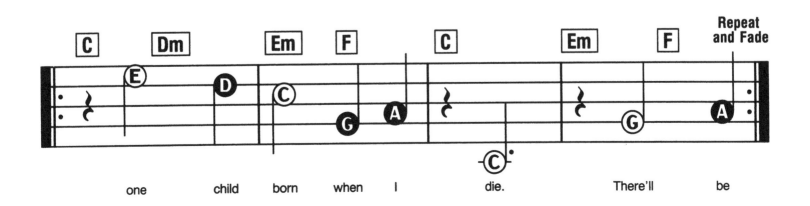

Angel of the Morning

Registration 1
Rhythm: Rock

Words and Music by
Chip Taylor

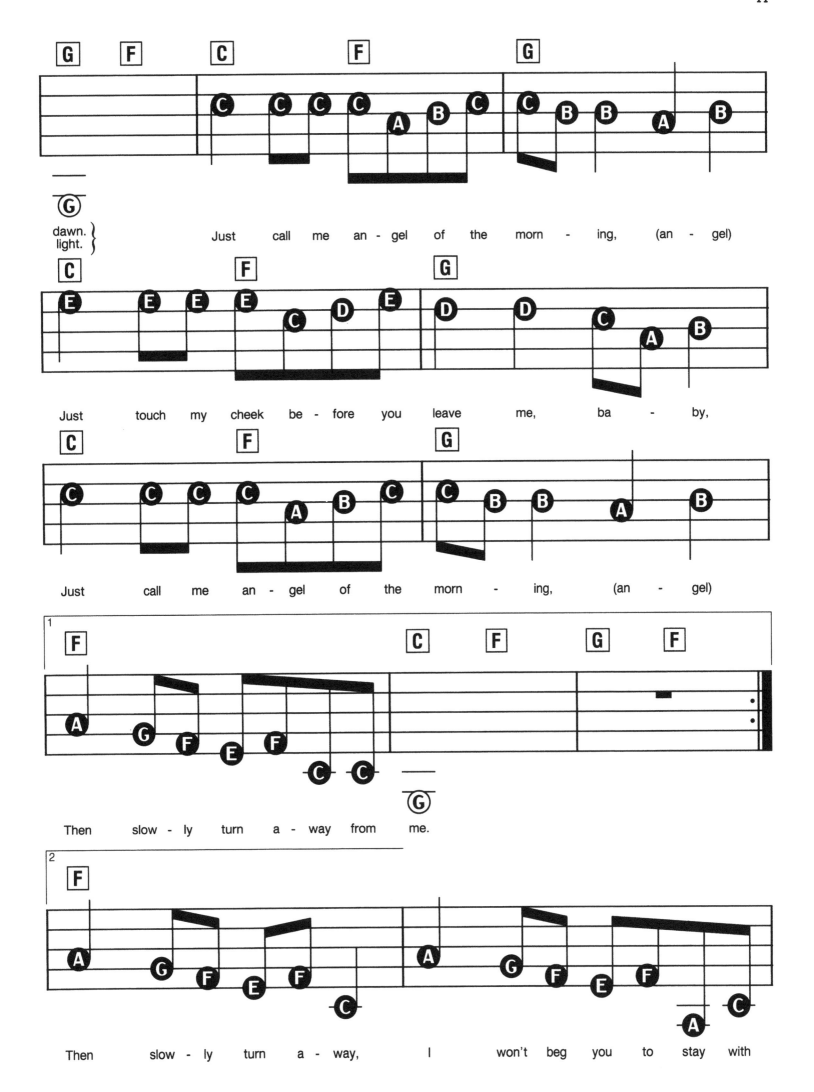

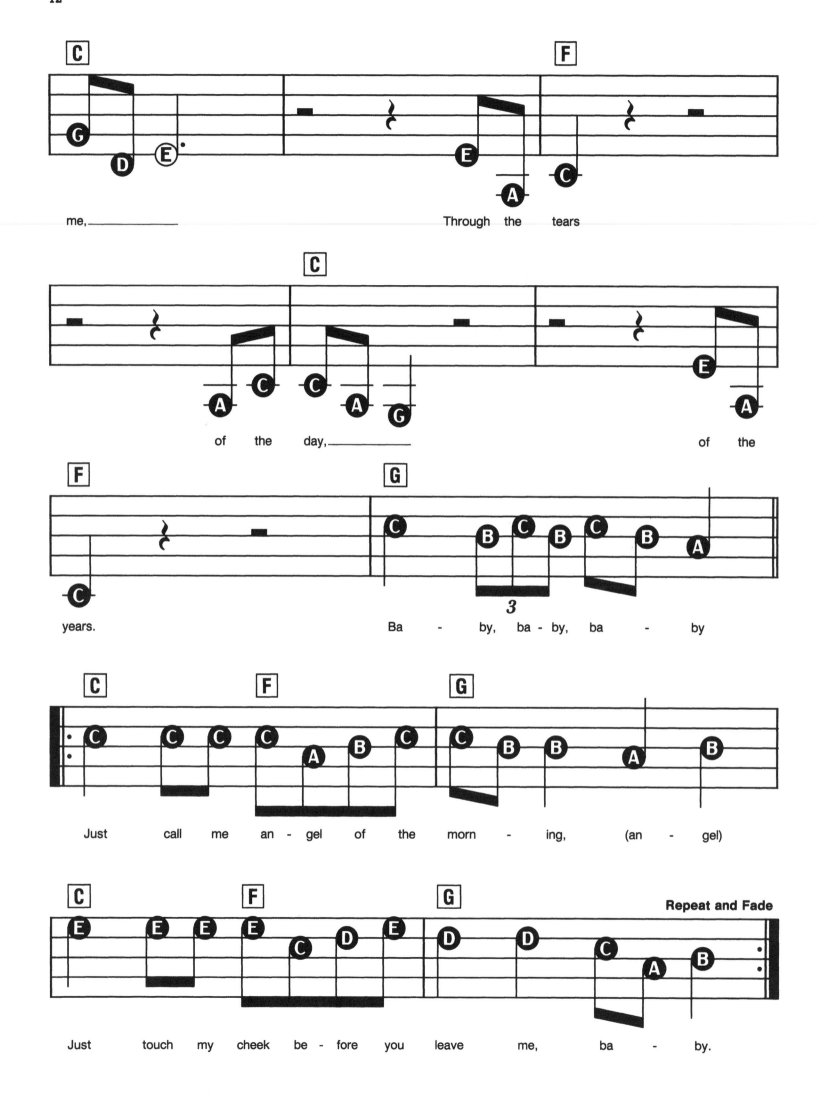

Blue Velvet

Registration 1
Rhythm: Fox Trot or Swing

Words and Music by Bernie Wayne
and Lee Morris

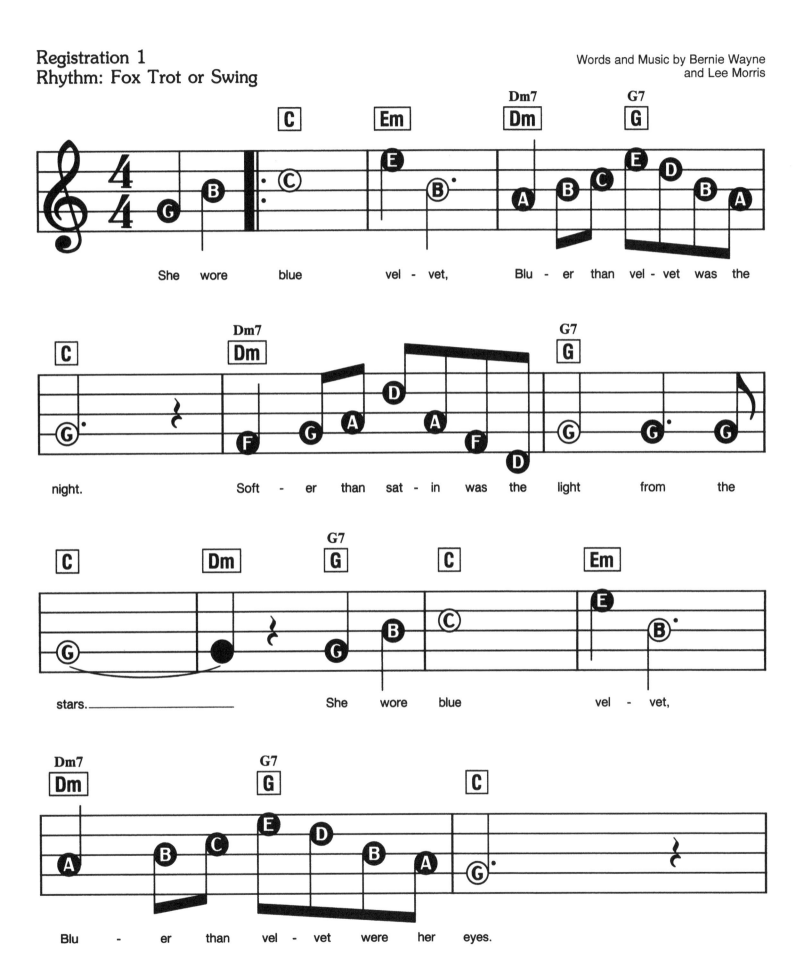

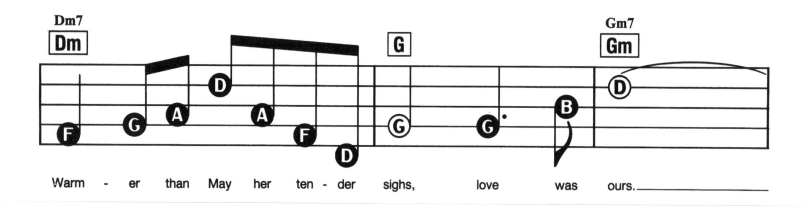

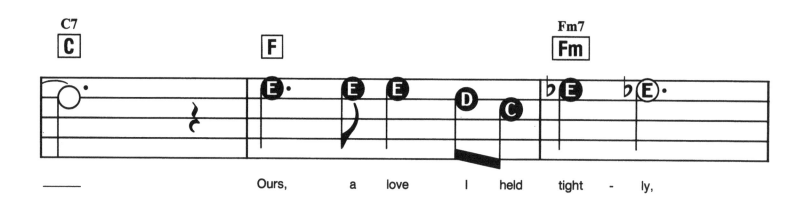

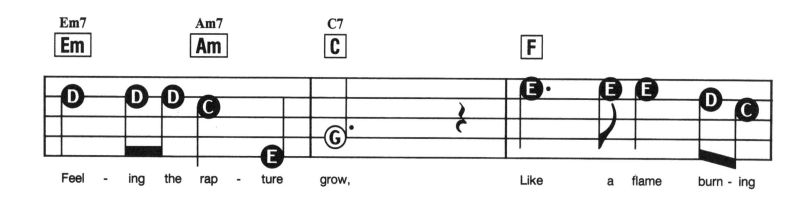

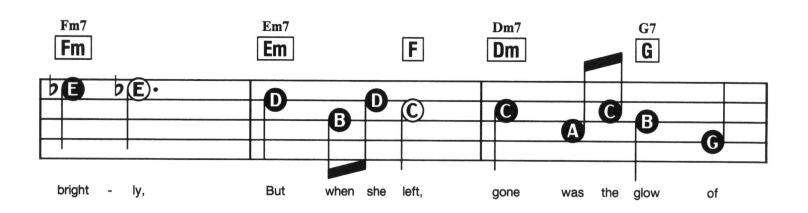

15

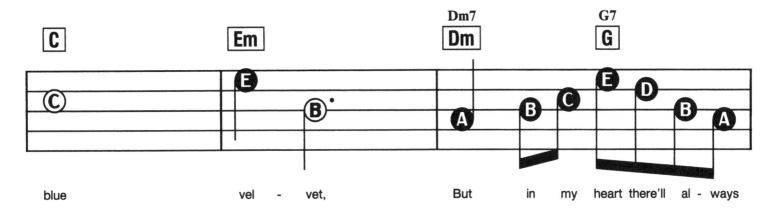

blue vel - vet, But in my heart there'll al - ways

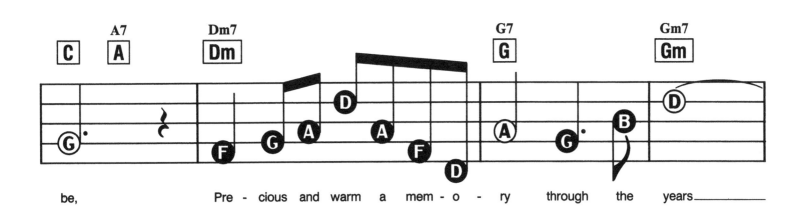

be, Pre - cious and warm a mem - o - ry through the years_____

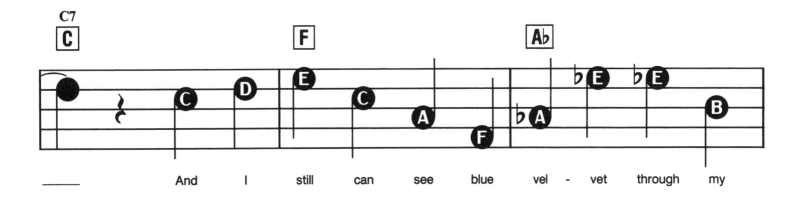

_____ And I still can see blue vel - vet through my

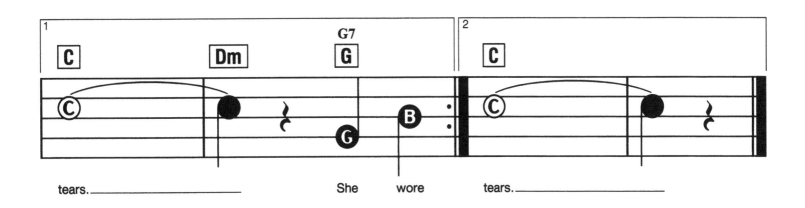

tears._____ She wore tears._____

The Boy from New York City

Registration 2
Rhythm: Shuffle or Swing

Words and Music by John Taylor
and George Davis

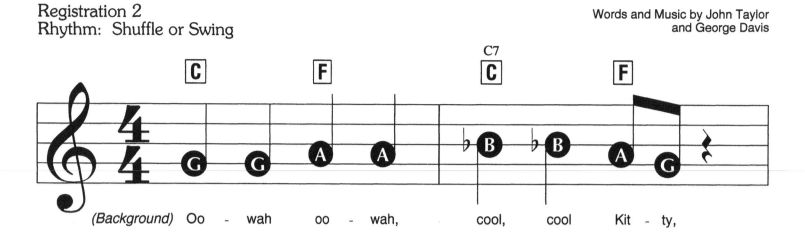

(Background) Oo - wah oo - wah, cool, cool Kit - ty,

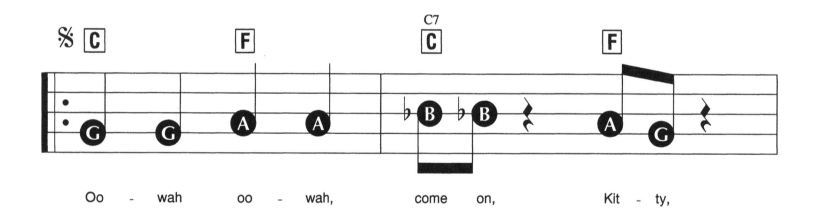

Tell us a - bout the boy from New York Ci - ty.

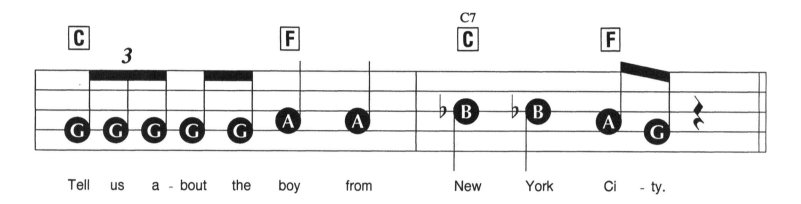

Oo - wah oo - wah, come on, Kit - ty,

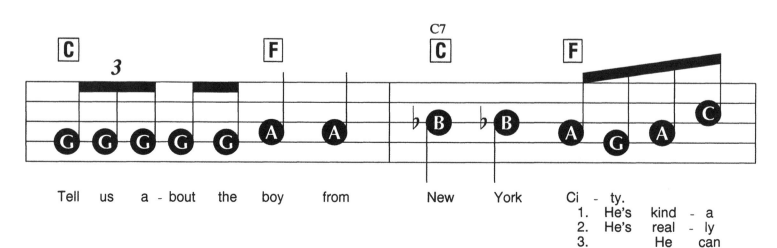

Tell us a - bout the boy from New York Ci - ty.

1. He's kind - a
2. He's real - ly
3. He can

17

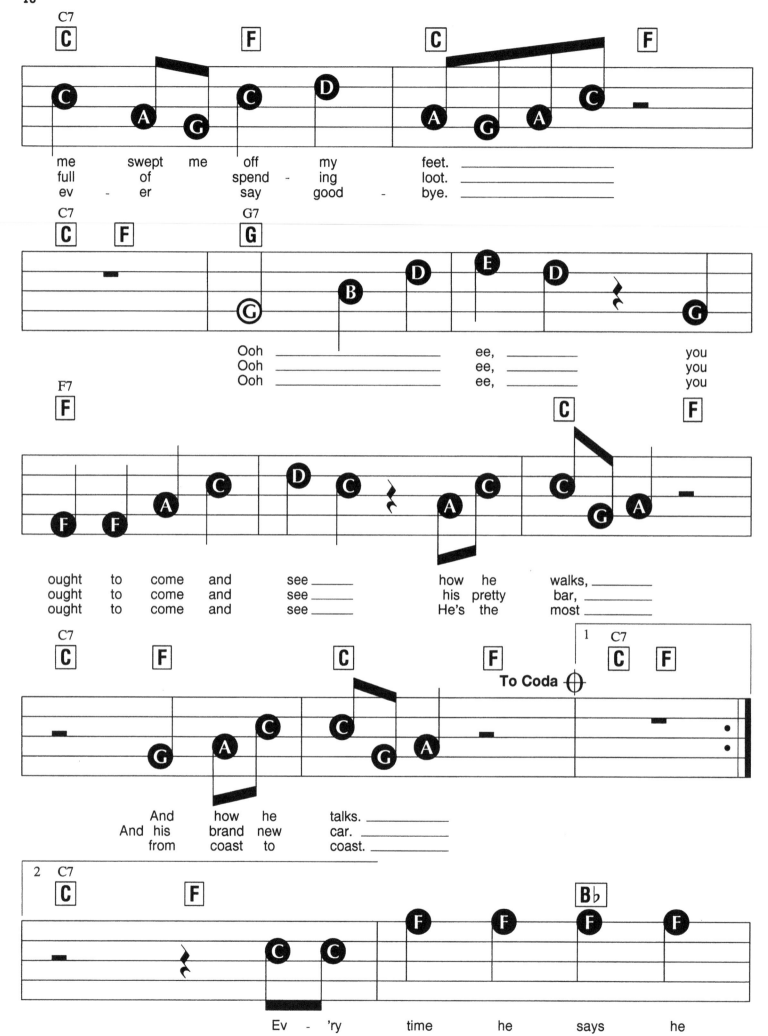

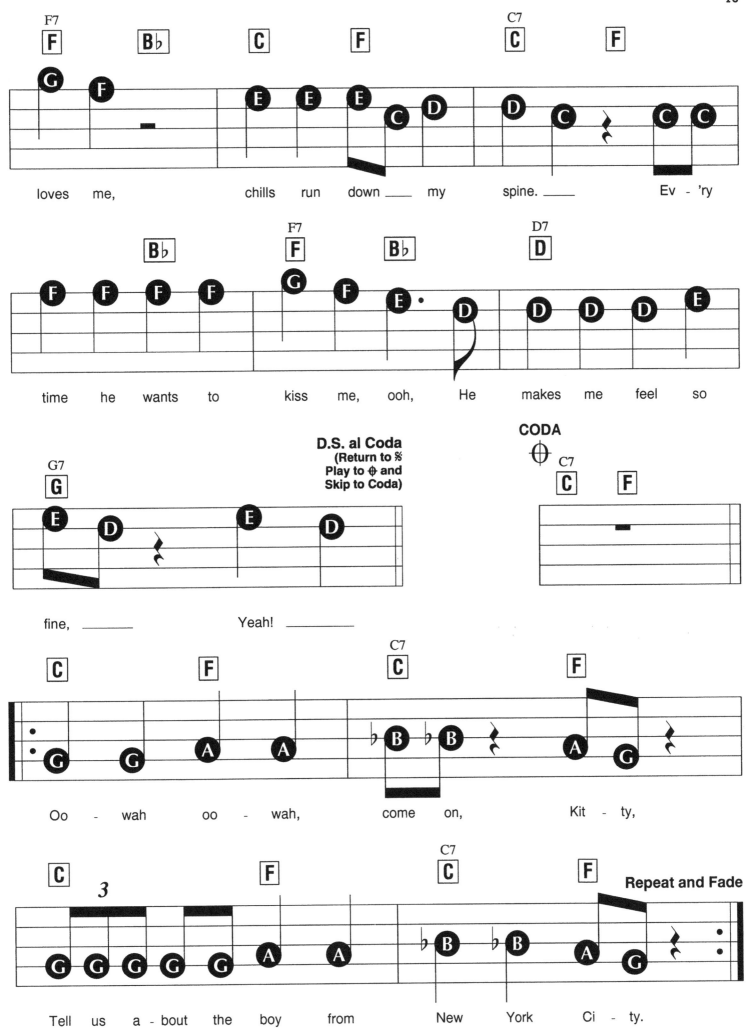

Crying

Registration 3
Rhythm: Country Ballad

Words and Music by Roy Orbison
and Joe Melson

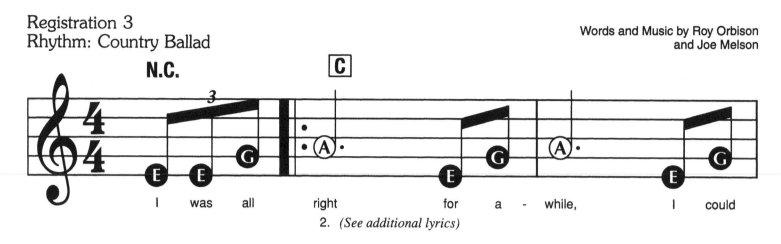

I was all right for a - while, I could

2. *(See additional lyrics)*

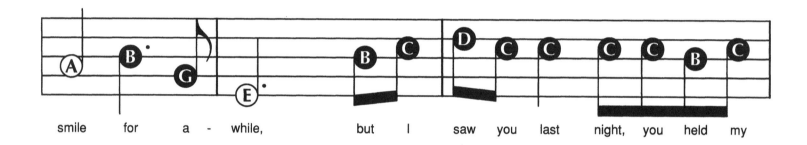

smile for a - while, but I saw you last night, you held my

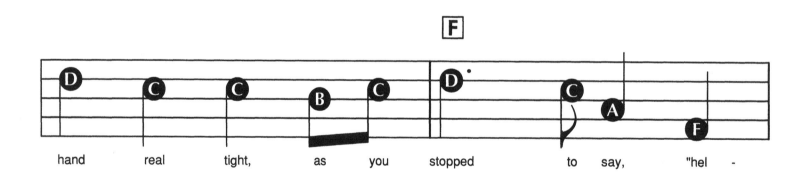

hand real tight, as you stopped to say, "hel -

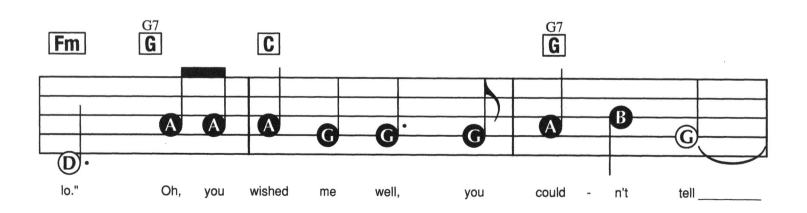

lo." Oh, you wished me well, you could - n't tell _____

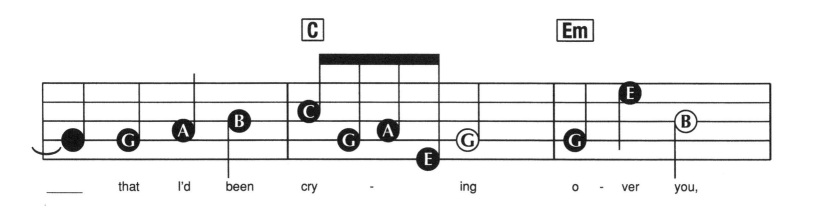

that I'd been cry - ing o - ver you,

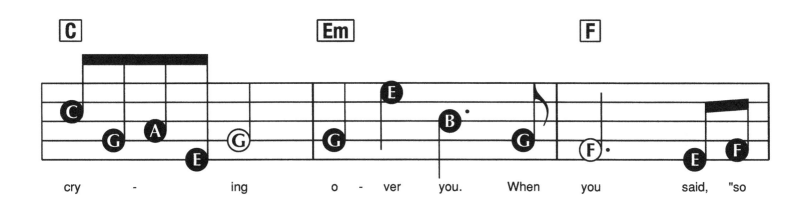

cry - ing o - ver you. When you said, "so

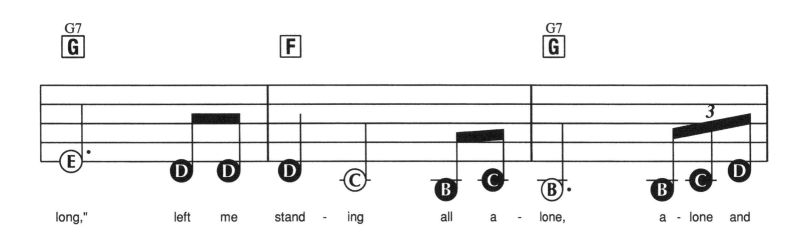

long," left me stand - ing all a - lone, a - lone and

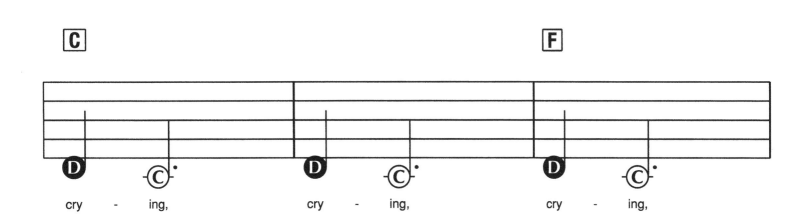

cry - ing, cry - ing, cry - ing,

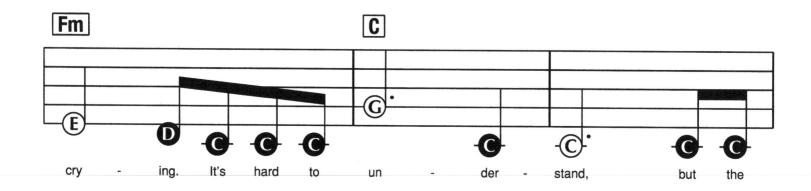

cry - ing. It's hard to un - der - stand, but the

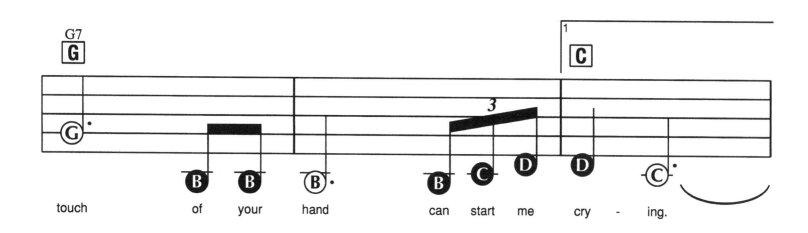

touch of your hand can start me cry - ing.

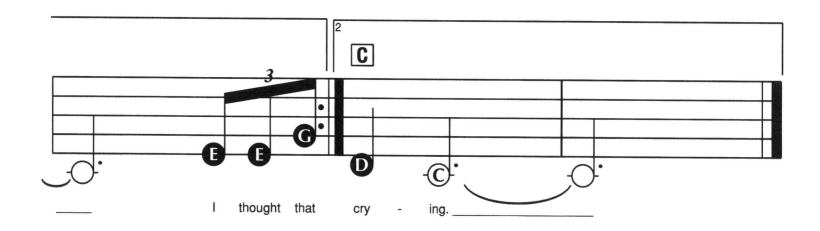

_____ I thought that cry - ing. _____

Additional Lyrics

2   I thought that I was over you,
    But it's true, so true:
    I love you even more than I did before.
    But darling, what can I do?
    For you don't love me and I'll always be
    Crying over you, crying over you.
    Yes, now you're gone and from this moment on
    I'll be crying, crying, crying, crying,
    Yeah, crying, crying over you.

Dancing in the Street

Registration 5
Rhythm: Rock or 8 Beat

Words and Music by Marvin Gaye,
Ivy Hunter and William Stevenson

F7

Call - ing out a - round the world are you
in - vi - ta - tion across the na - tion you a

rea - dy for a brand new beat
chance _____ for _____ folks to meet there'll

sum - mer's here _____ and the time is right for
be laugh - ing sing - ing and mu - sic swinging

danc - ing in the street. They're danc - ing in Chi -
danc - ing in the street. Phila - del - phia, P. A.,

ca - go, _____
Baltimore and down in D. C. Now
New Or - leans,

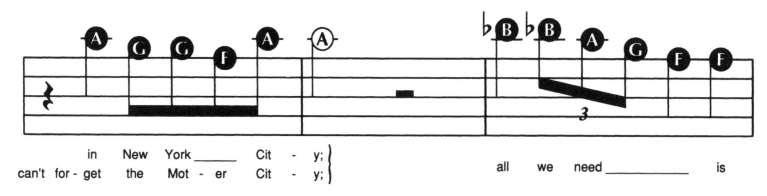

in New York _____ Cit - y; }
can't for - get the Mot - er Cit - y; }
all we need _____ is

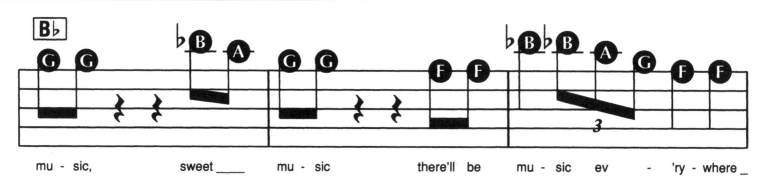

mu - sic, sweet ____ mu - sic there'll be mu - sic ev - 'ry - where _

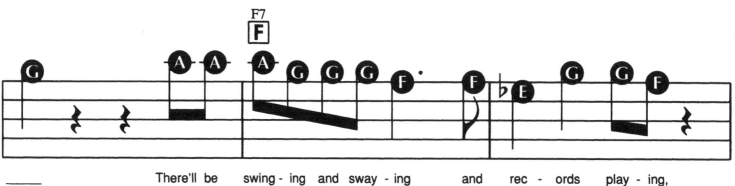

_____ There'll be swing - ing and sway - ing and rec - ords play - ing,

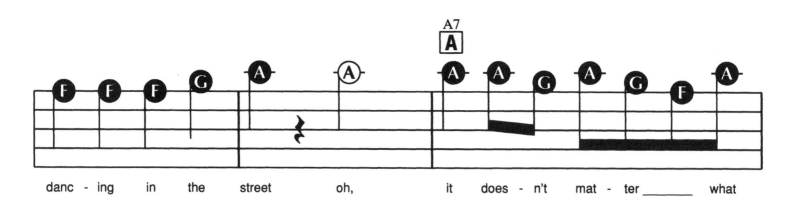

danc - ing in the street oh, it does - n't mat - ter _____ what

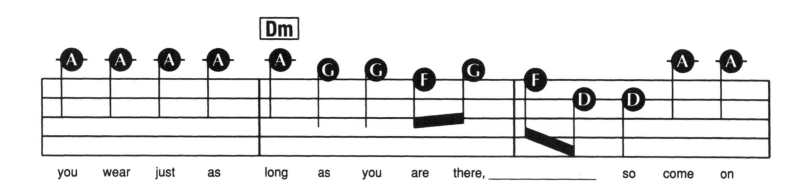

you wear just as long as you are there, _____ so come on

25

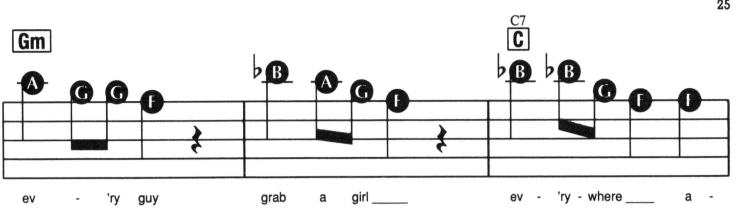

ev - 'ry guy   grab a girl _____   ev - 'ry - where ____ a -

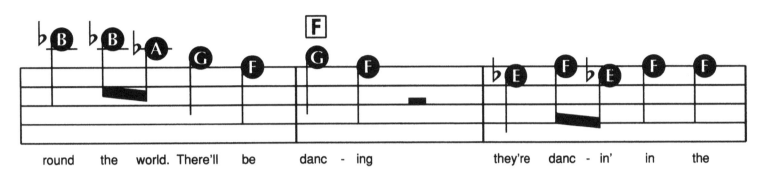

round   the   world. There'll   be   danc - ing   they're danc - in'   in   the

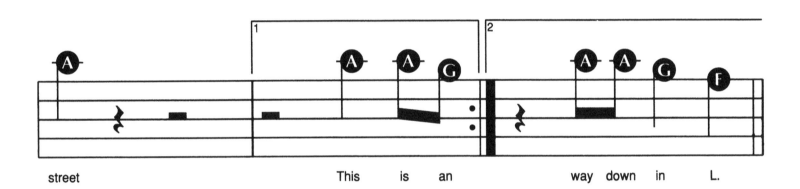

street   This   is   an   way down in   L.

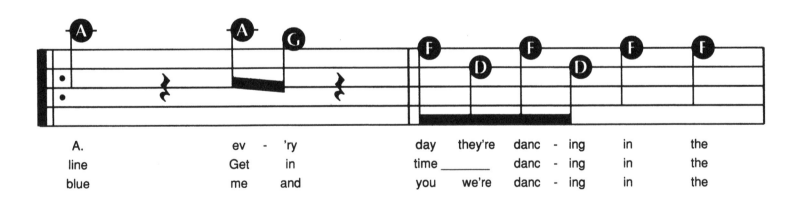

A.   ev - 'ry   day   they're danc - ing   in   the
line   Get   in   time _____ danc - ing   in   the
blue   me   and   you   we're danc - ing   in   the

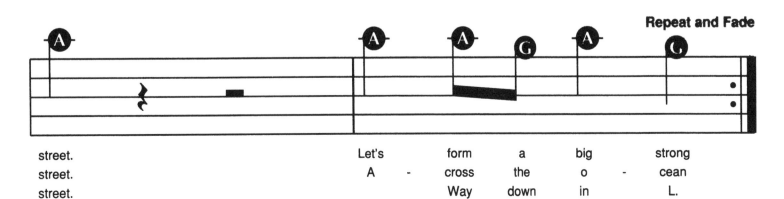

street.   Let's   form   a   big   strong
street.   A - cross   the   o - cean
street.   Way   down   in   L.

Daydream Believer

featured in the Television Series THE MONKEES

Registration 1
Rhythm: Fox Trot or Swing

Words and Music by
John Stewart

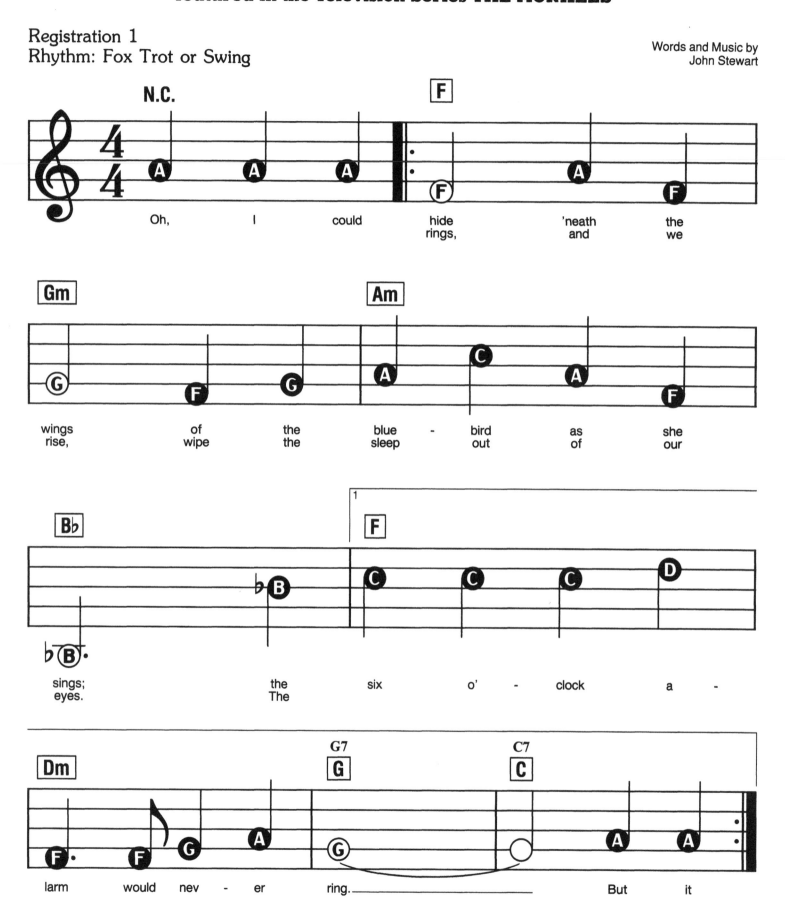

28

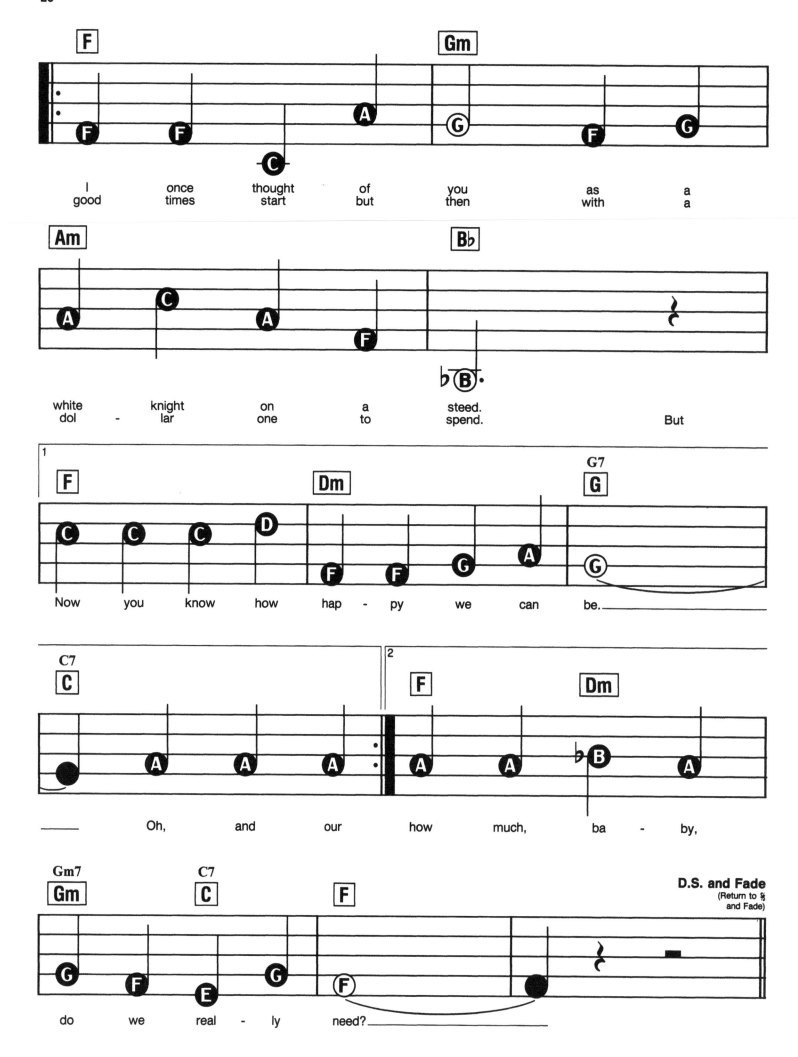

Do You Love Me

Registration 7
Rhythm: Rock or 8-Beat

Words and Music by
Berry Gordy

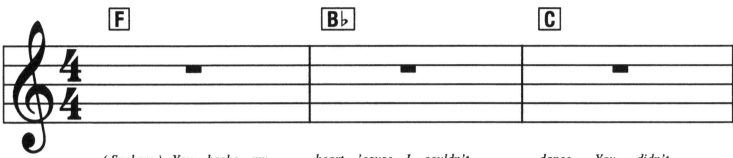

(Spoken:) You broke my heart 'cause I couldn't dance. You didn't

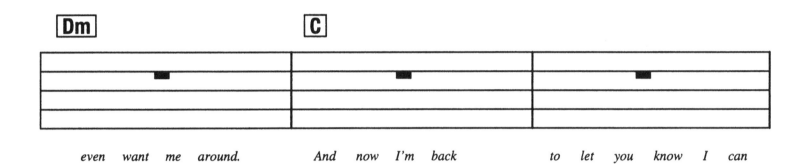

even want me around. And now I'm back to let you know I can

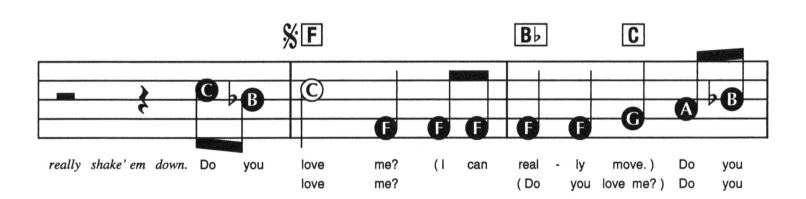

really shake 'em down. Do you love me? (I can real - ly move.) Do you
love me? (Do you love me?) Do you

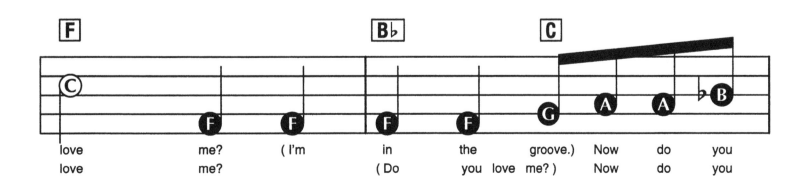

love me? (I'm in the groove.) Now do you
love me? (Do you love me?) Now do you

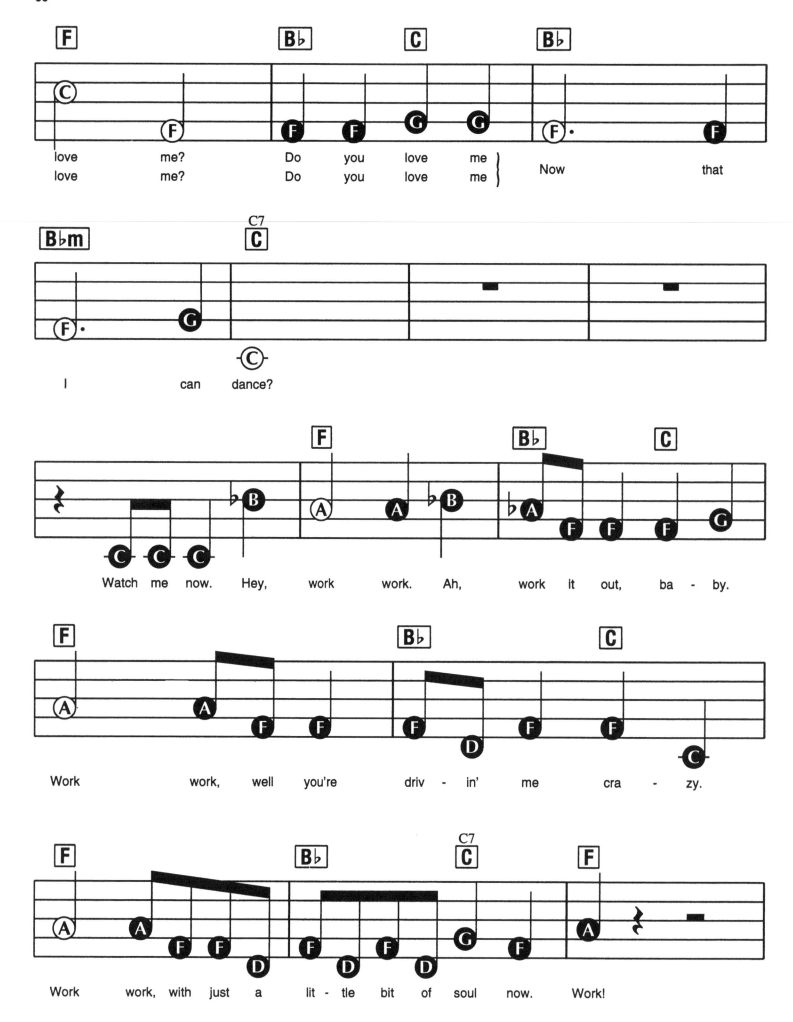

Different Drum

Registration 9
Rhythm: Rock or 8 Beat

Words and Music by Michael Nesmith

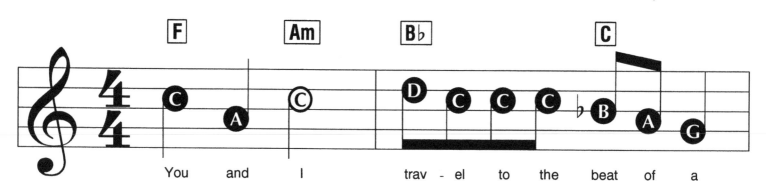

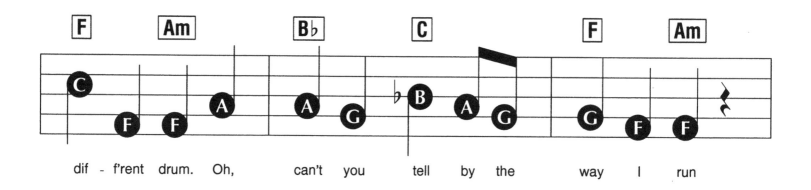

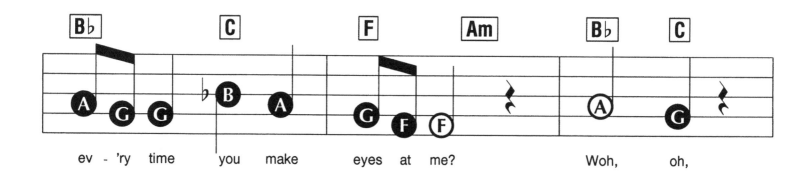

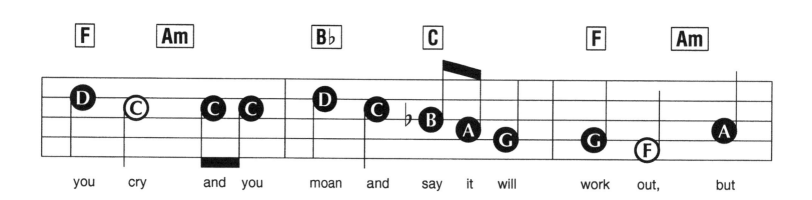

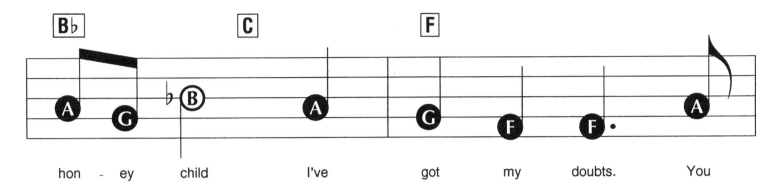

hon - ey child   I've   got   my   doubts.   You

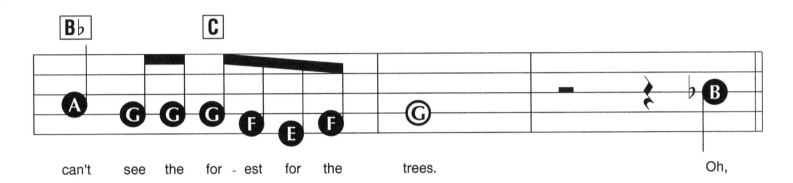

can't   see   the   for - est   for   the   trees.   Oh,

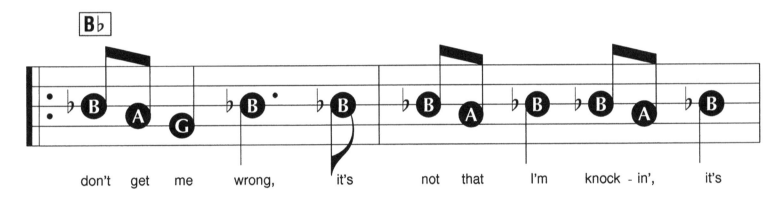

don't   get   me   wrong,   it's   not   that   I'm   knock - in',   it's

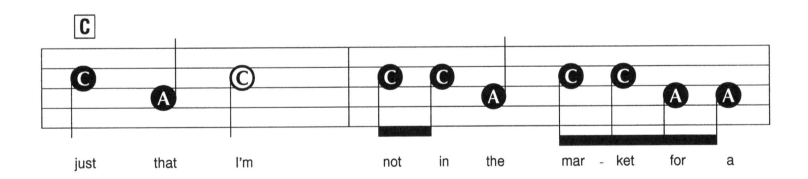

just   that   I'm   not   in   the   mar - ket   for   a

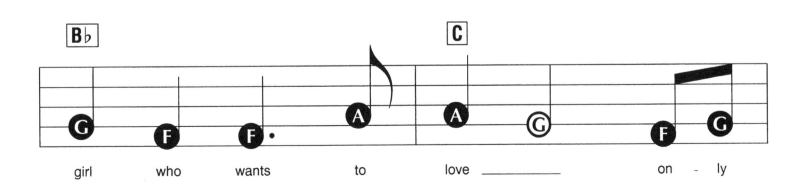

girl   who   wants   to   love _____ on - ly

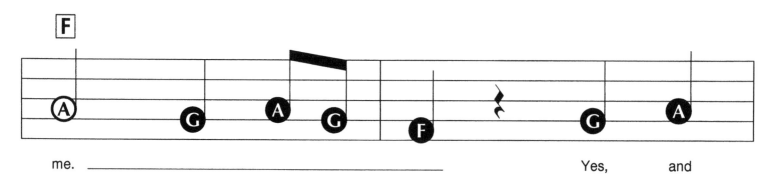

me. _____ Yes,   and

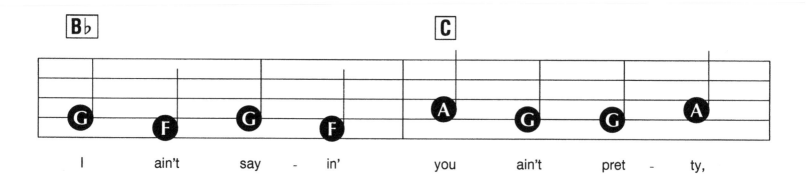

I   ain't   say - in'   you   ain't   pret - ty,

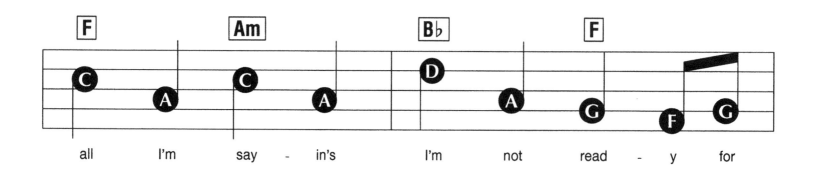

all   I'm   say - in's   I'm   not   read - y   for

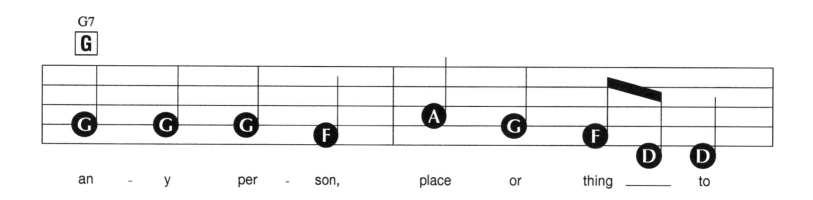

an - y   per - son,   place   or   thing _____ to

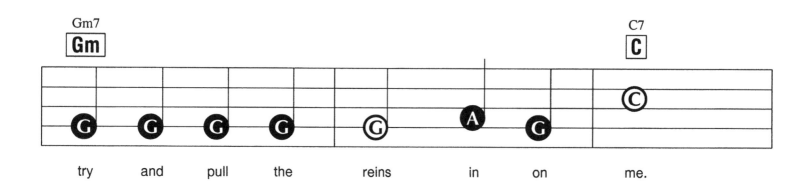

try   and   pull   the   reins   in   on   me.

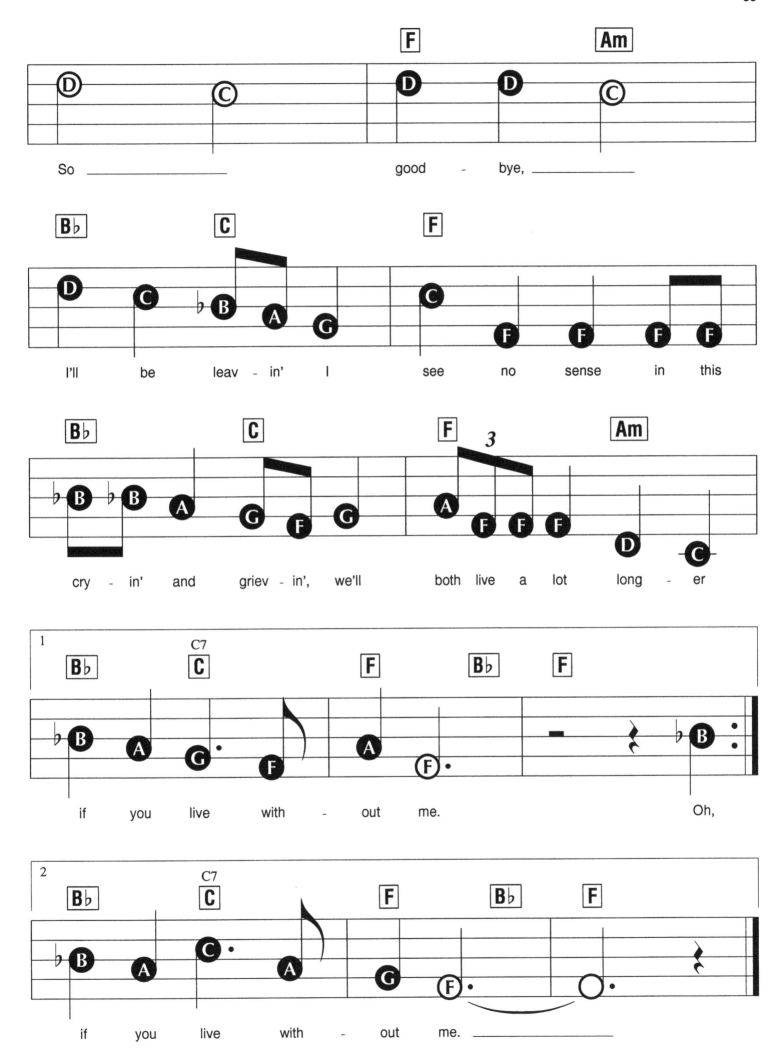

Do Wah Diddy Diddy

Registration 5
Rhythm: Rock or Pops

Words and Music by Jeff Barry
and Ellie Greenwich

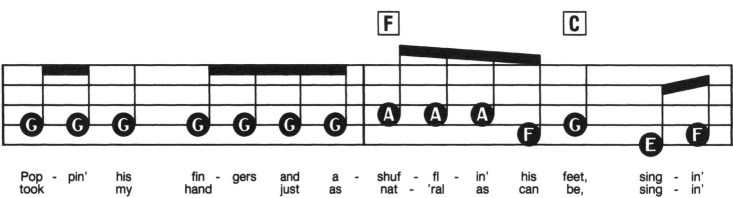

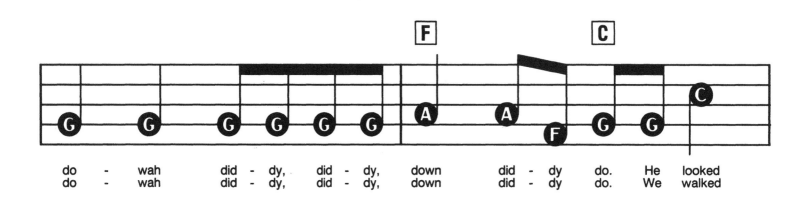

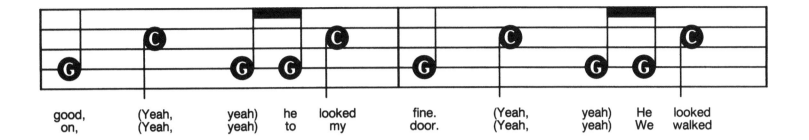

good, (Yeah, yeah) he looked fine. (Yeah, yeah) He looked
on, (Yeah, yeah) to my door. (Yeah, yeah) We walked

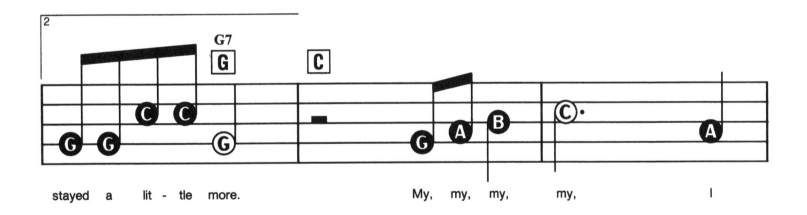

good, he looked fine, and I near - ly lost my mind. Be -
on to my door, and he

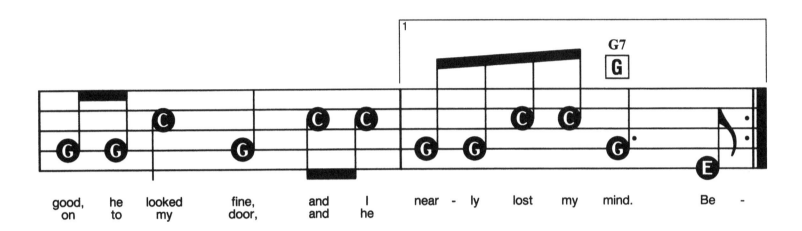

stayed a lit - tle more. My, my, my, my, I

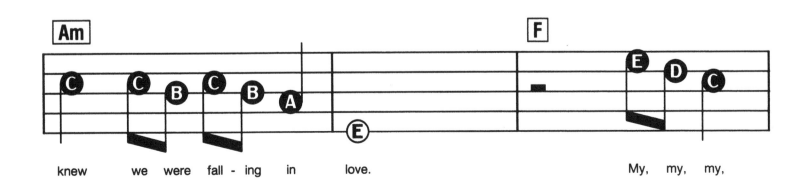

knew we were fall - ing in love. My, my, my,

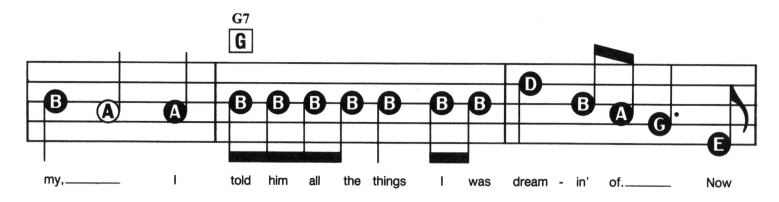

my,_____ I told him all the things I was dream - in' of._____ Now

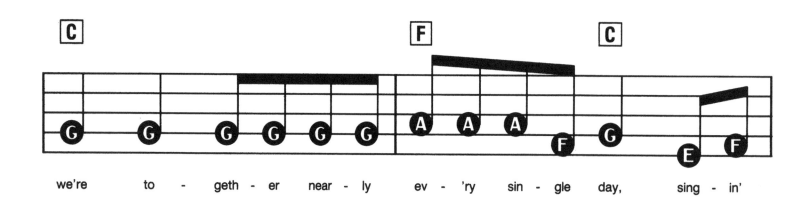

we're to - geth - er near - ly ev - 'ry sin - gle day, sing - in'

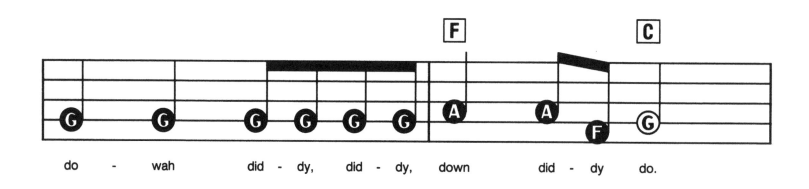

do - wah did - dy, did - dy, down did - dy do.

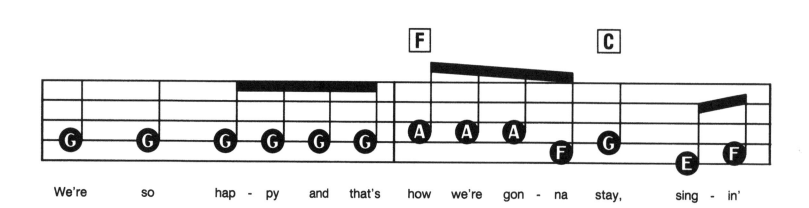

We're so hap - py and that's how we're gon - na stay, sing - in'

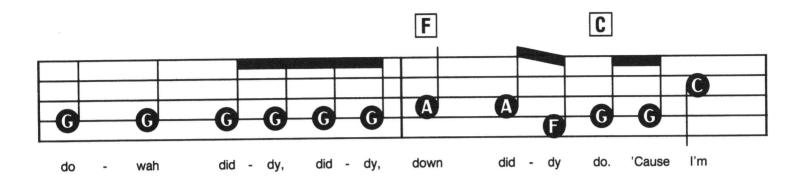

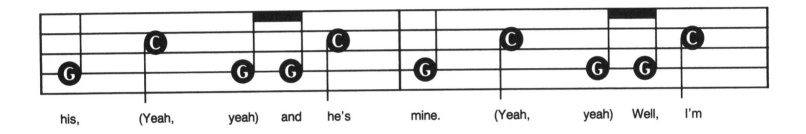

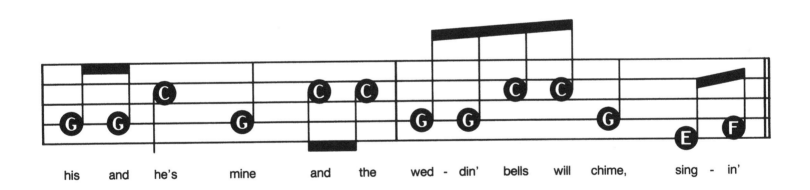

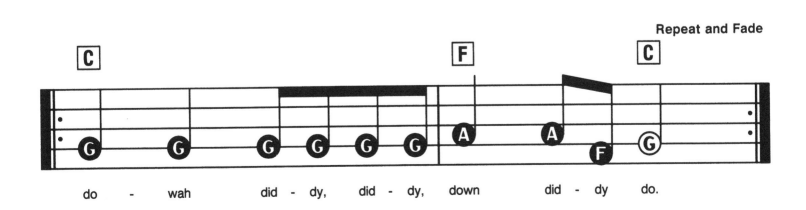

Downtown

Registration 5
Rhythm: Rock

Words and Music by
Tony Hatch

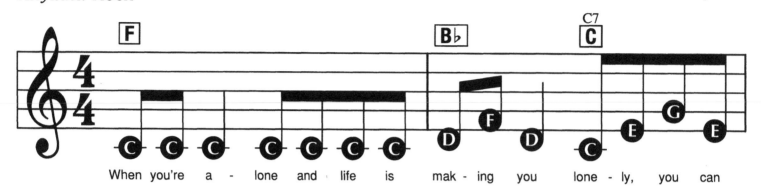

When you're a - lone and life is mak - ing you lone - ly, you can

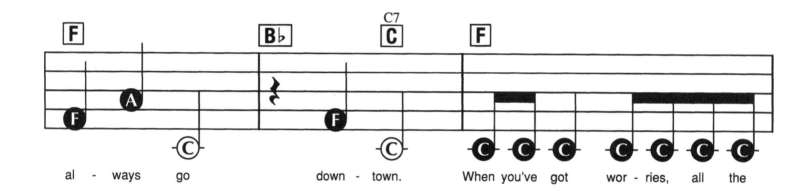

al - ways go down - town. When you've got wor - ries, all the

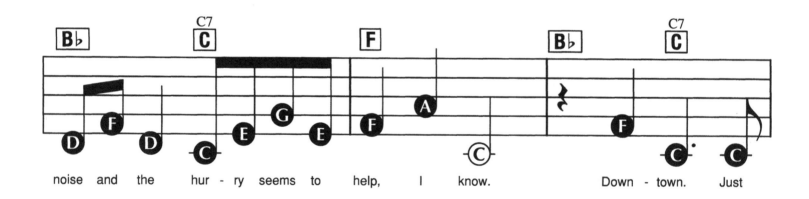

noise and the hur - ry seems to help, I know. Down - town. Just

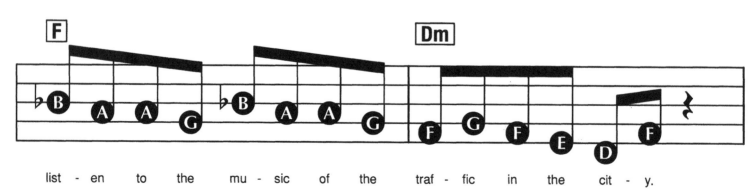

list - en to the mu - sic of the traf - fic in the cit - y.

MCA music publishing

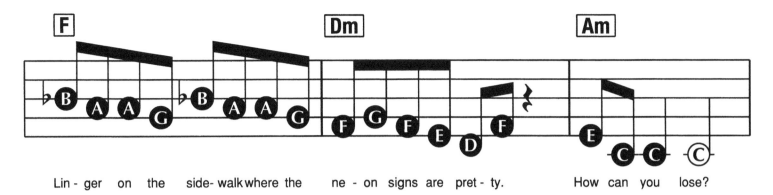

Lin - ger on the side- walk where the ne - on signs are pret - ty. How can you lose?

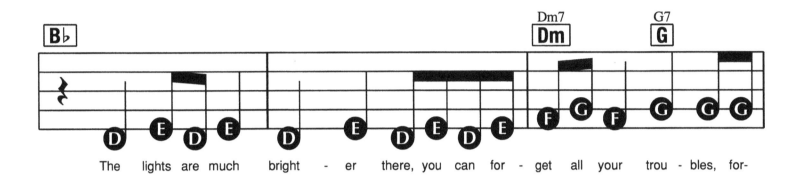

The lights are much bright - er there, you can for - get all your trou - bles, for-

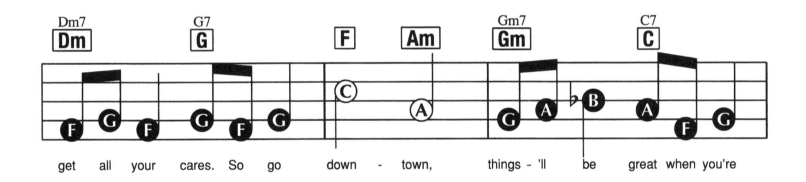

get all your cares. So go down - town, things - 'll be great when you're

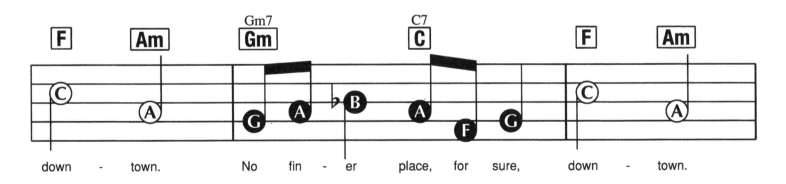

down - town. No fin - er place, for sure, down - town.

Repeat and Fade

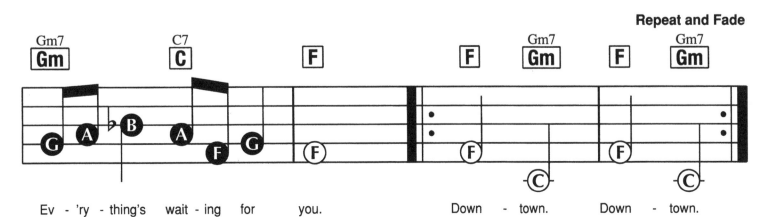

Ev - 'ry - thing's wait - ing for you. Down - town. Down - town.

Dream Baby
(How Long Must I Dream)

Registration 7
Rhythm: Ballad or Fox Trot

Words and Music by
Cindy Walker

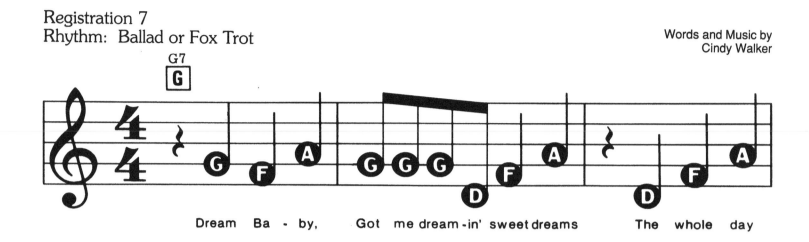

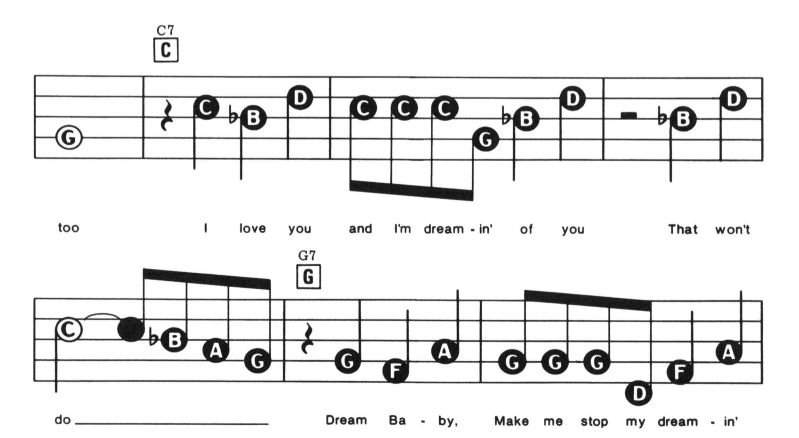

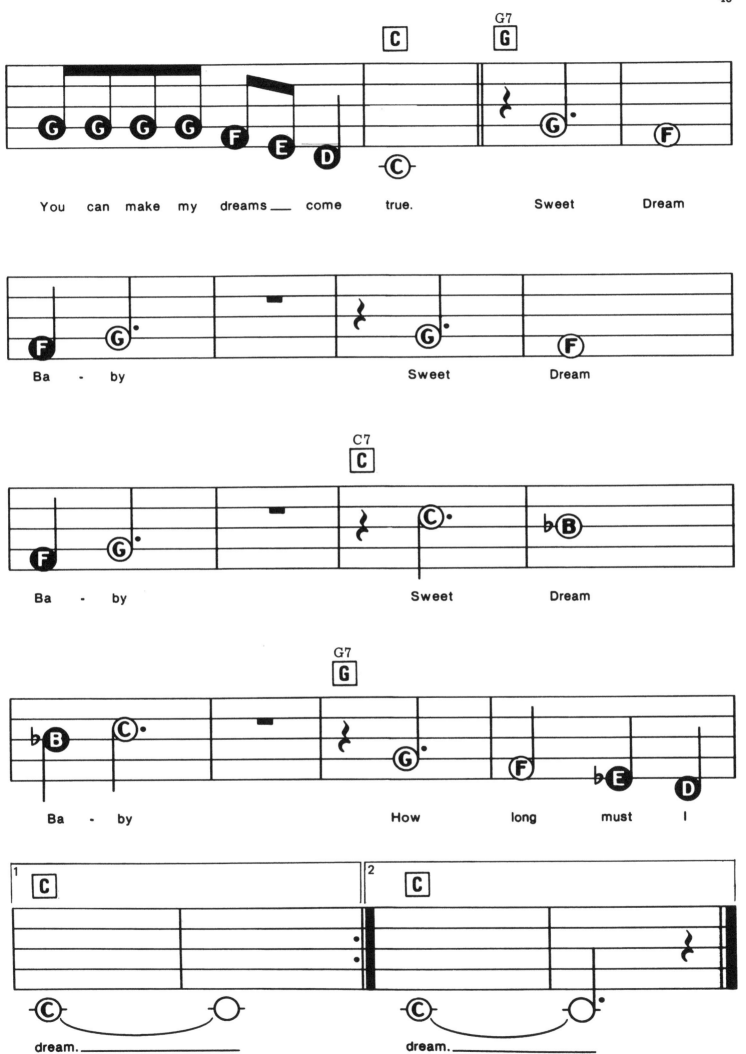

For Once in My Life

Registration 8
Rhythm: Rock or Pops

Lyric by Ronald Miller
Music by Orlando Murden

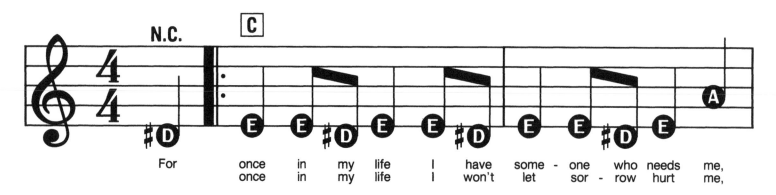

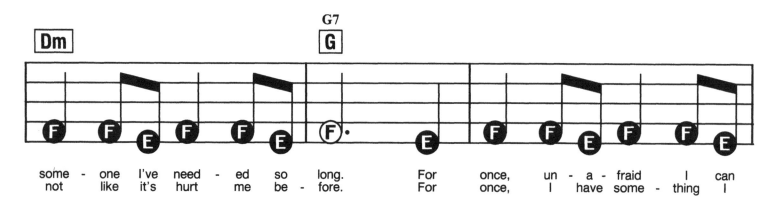

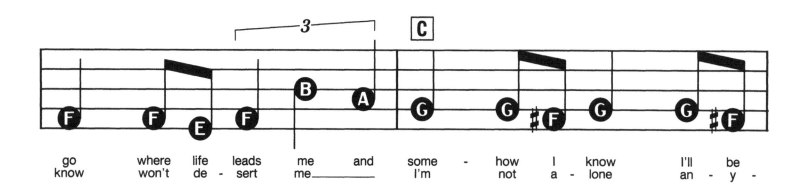

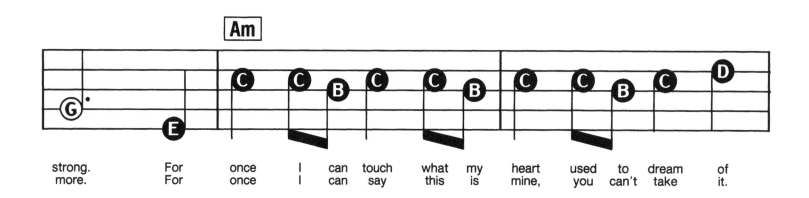

Gentle on My Mind

Registration 10
Rhythm: Fox Trot or Pops

Words and Music by
John Hartford

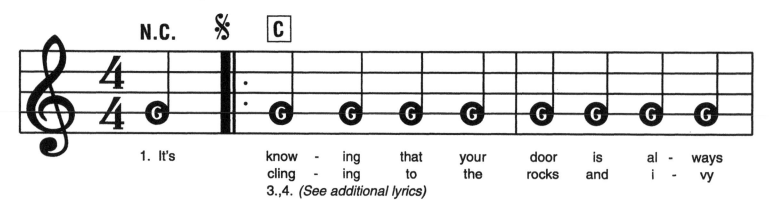

1. It's .... know - ing that your door is al - ways
   cling - ing to the rocks and i - vy
3.,4. *(See additional lyrics)*

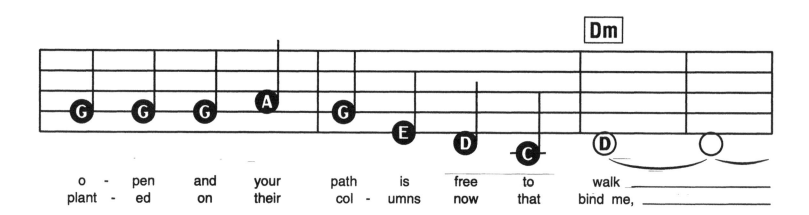

o - pen and your path is free to walk _____
plant - ed on their col - umns now that bind me, _____

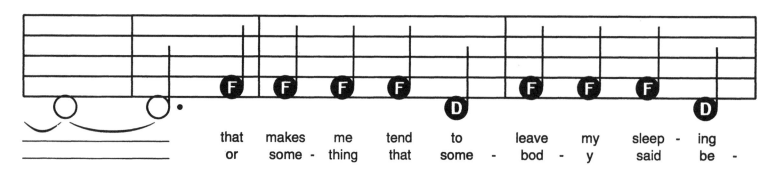

_____ that makes me tend to leave my sleep - ing
_____ or some - thing that some - bod - y said be -

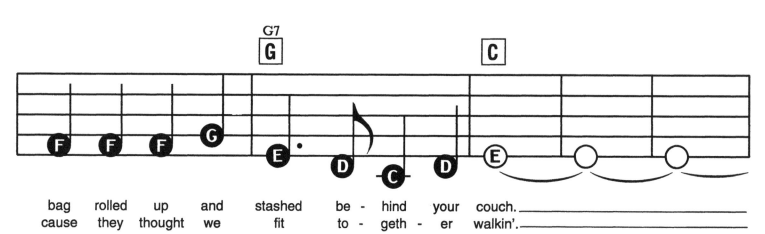

bag rolled up and stashed be - hind your couch. _____
cause they thought we fit to - geth - er walkin'. _____

3

C

2. It's not   mind.
3. Though the

D.S. al Coda
(Return to %
Play to ⊕ and
Skip to Coda)

4. I

CODA
⊕

cupped hands round   a   tin   can,   I   pre - tend   to   hold   you

Dm

to   my   breast   and   find

that   you're   wav - in'   from   the

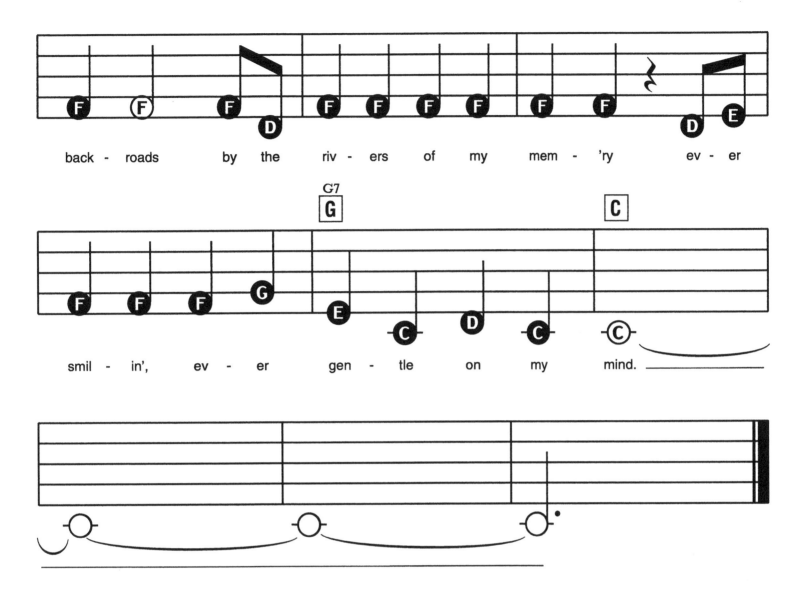

back - roads by the riv - ers of my mem - 'ry ev - er

G7

smil - in', ev - er gen - tle on my mind. _____

Additional Lyrics

3. Though the wheat fields and the clotheslines
   and the junkyards and the highways come between us,
   and some other woman cryin' to her mother
   'cause she turned and I was gone.
   I still might run in silence,
   tears of joy might stain my face,
   and the summer sun might burn me till I'm blind,
   but not to where I cannot see you
   walkin' on the backroads
   by the rivers flowing gentle on my mind.

4. I dip my cup of soup back from some gurglin',
   cracklin' cauldron in some train yard,
   my beard a rough'ning coal pile and
   a dirty hat pulled low across my face.
   Through cupped hands round a tin can,
   I pretend to hold you to my breast and find
   that you're wavin' from the backroads
   by the rivers of my mem'ry,
   ever smilin', ever gentle on my mind.

Goin' Out of My Head

Registration 7
Rhythm: Latin or Beguine

Words and Music by Teddy Randazzo
and Bobby Weinstein

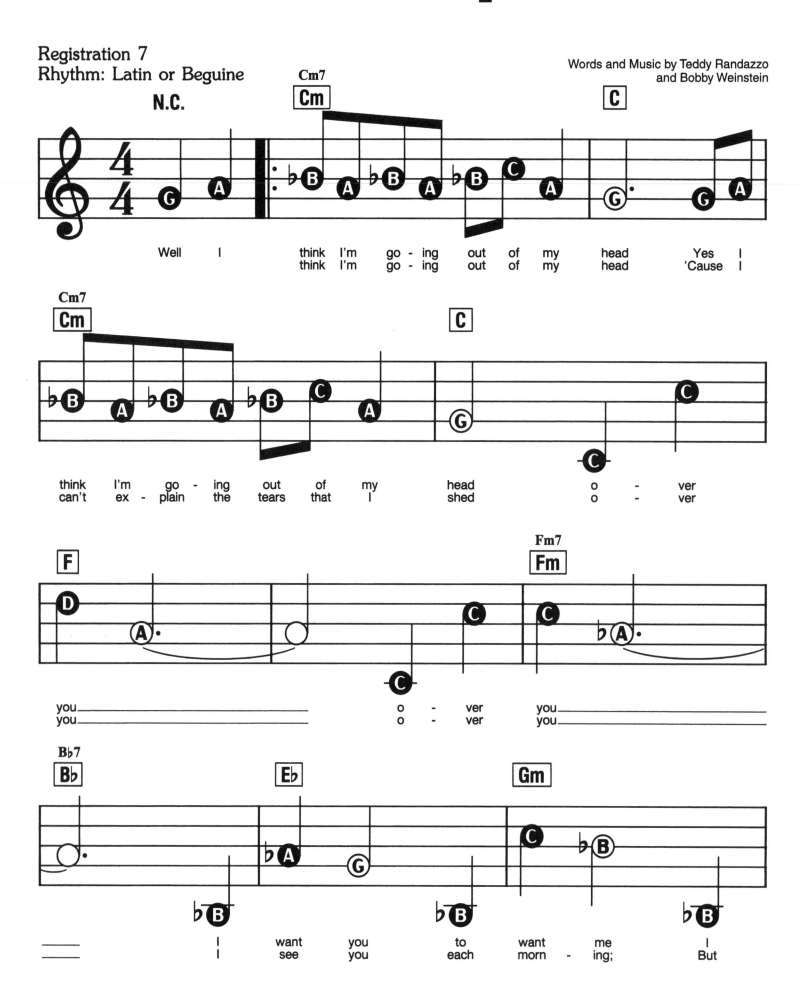

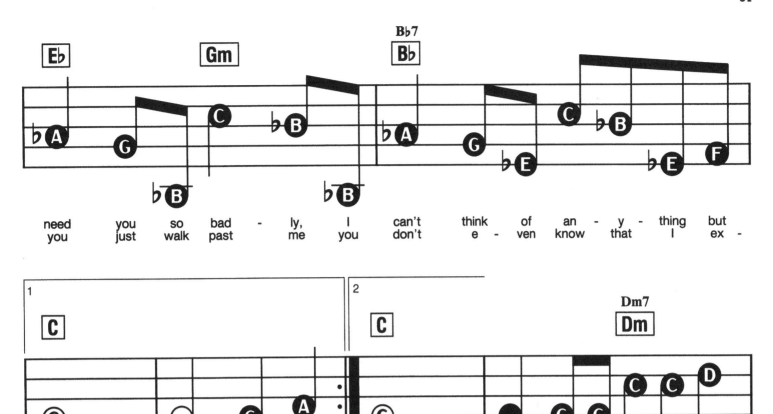

need you so bad - ly, I can't think of an - y - thing but
you just walk past me you don't e - ven know that I ex -

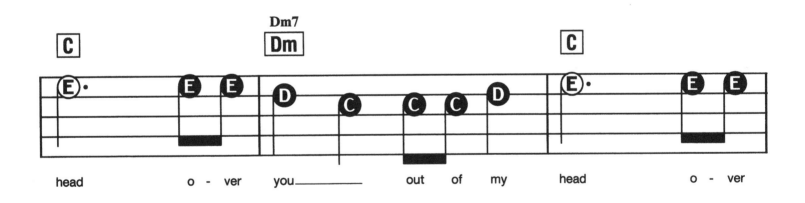

you_____ And I
ist_____ Go - in' out of my

head   o - ver you_____   out of my head   o - ver

you_____   out of my head   day and night,   Night and day   and

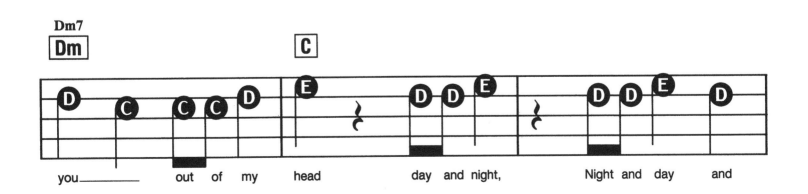

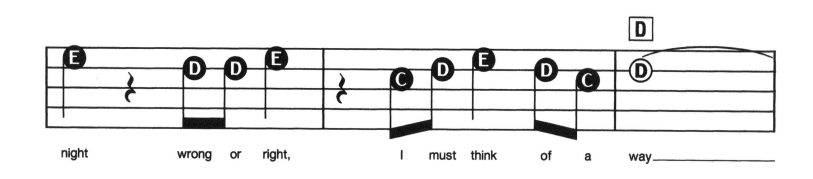

night   wrong or right,   I must think of a way

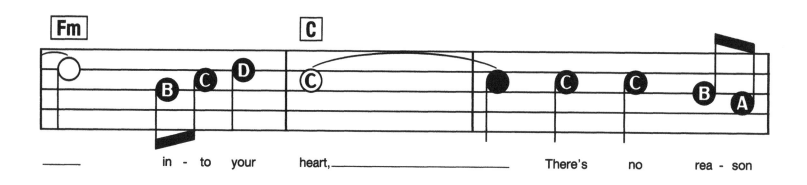

in - to your heart,   There's no rea - son

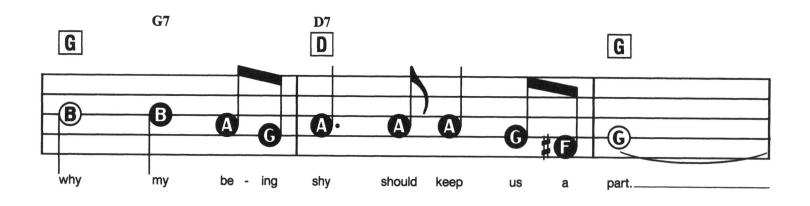

why my be - ing shy should keep us a part.

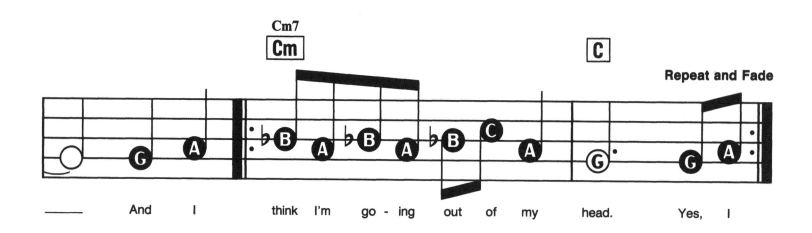

And I   think I'm go - ing out of my head.   Yes, I

Hurt So Bad

Registration 7
Rhythm: Pops or 8 Beat

Words and Music by Teddy Randazzo,
Bobby Hart and Bobby Weinstein

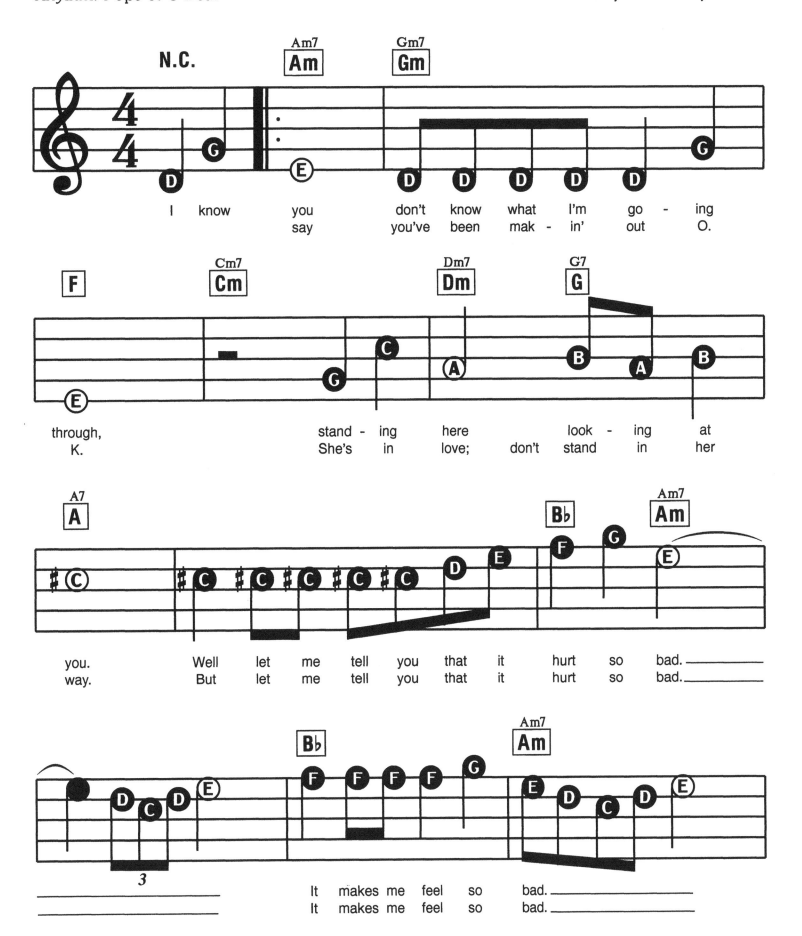

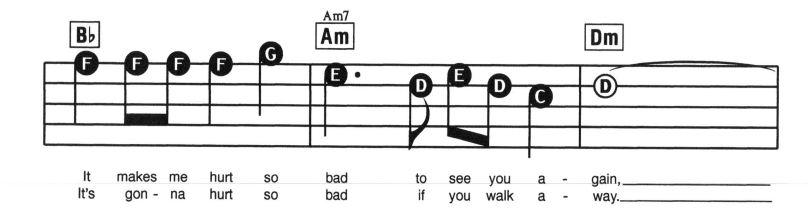

It makes me hurt so bad to see you a - gain,_____
It's gon - na hurt so bad if you walk a - way._____

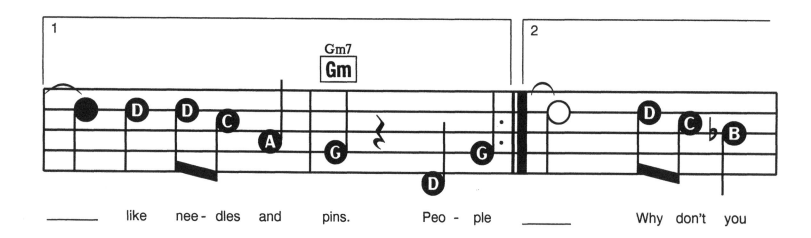

_____ like nee - dles and pins. Peo - ple _____ Why don't you

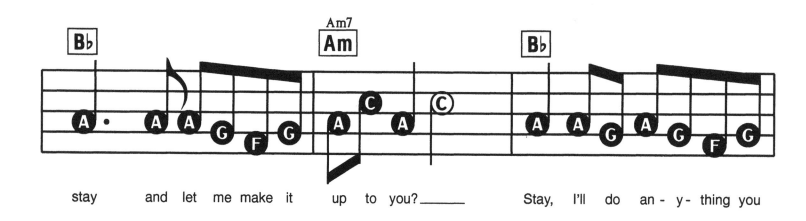

stay and let me make it up to you?_____ Stay, I'll do an - y - thing you

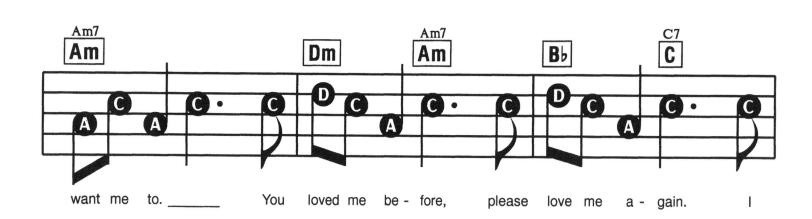

want me to. _____ You loved me be - fore, please love me a - gain. I

55

Heatwave
(Love Is Like a Heatwave)

Registration 4
Rhythm: Swing or Shuffle

Words and Music by Edward Holland,
Lamont Dozier and Brian Holland

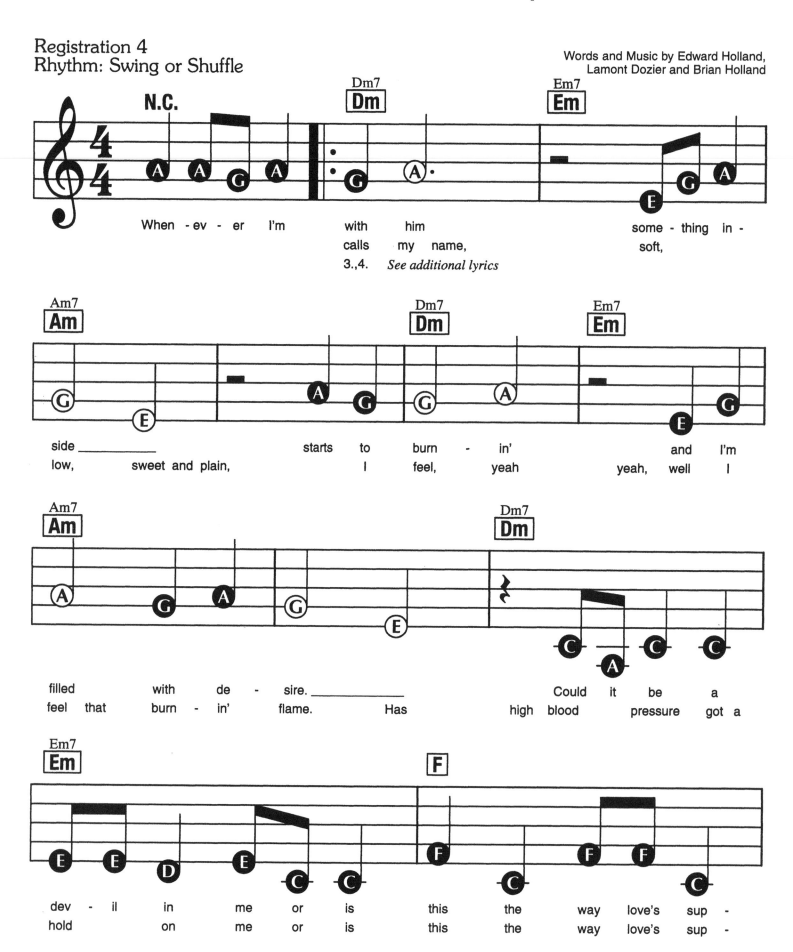

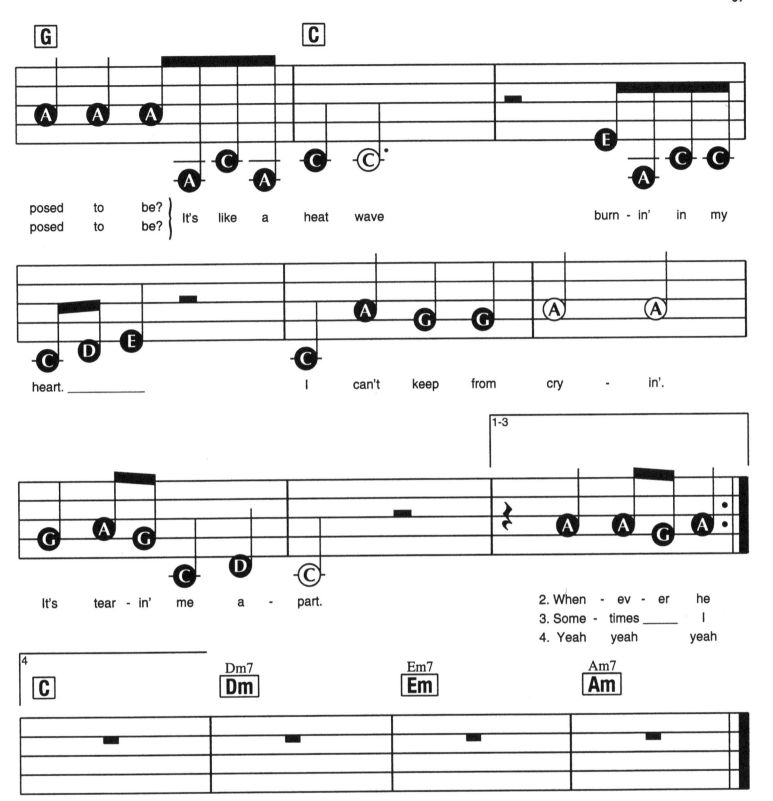

posed to be?
posed to be?

It's like a heat wave burn - in' in my heart. _____ I can't keep from cry - in'.

It's tear - in' me a - part.

1-3

2. When - ev - er he
3. Some - times _____ I
4. Yeah yeah yeah

4

C Dm7 Dm Em7 Em Am7 Am

Additional Lyrics

3. Sometimes I stare into space,
   tears all over my face.
   I can't explain it,
   Don't understand it.
   I ain't never felt like this before.
   Now that funny feelin' has me amazed.
   I don't know what to do, my head's in a haze.

4. Yeah yeah yeah yeah yeah
   yeah whoa ho.
   Yeah yeah yeah yeah ho.
   Don't pass up this chance.
   This time it's a true romance.

I Hear a Symphony

Registration 4
Rhythm: Swing or Shuffle

Words and Music by Edward Holland,
Lamont Dozier and Brian Holland

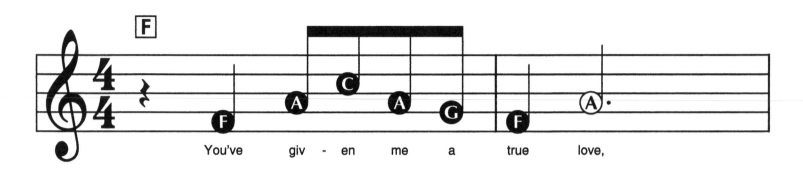

You've giv - en me a true love,

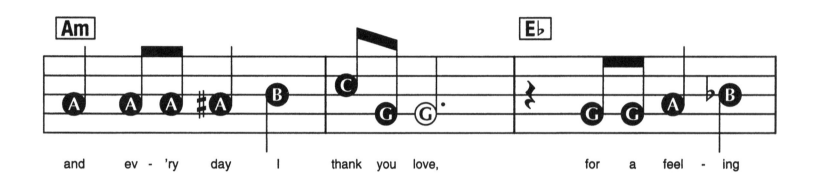

and ev - 'ry day I thank you love, for a feel - ing

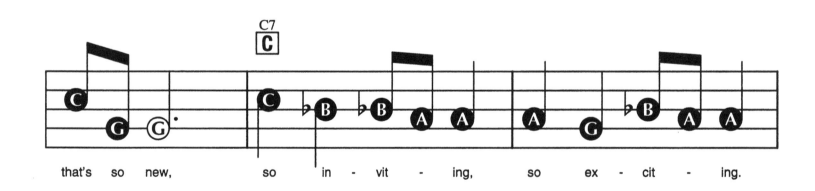

that's so new, so in - vit - ing, so ex - cit - ing.

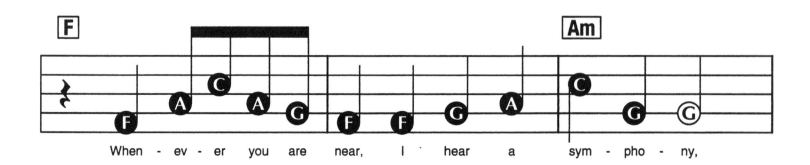

When - ev - er you are near, I hear a sym - pho - ny,

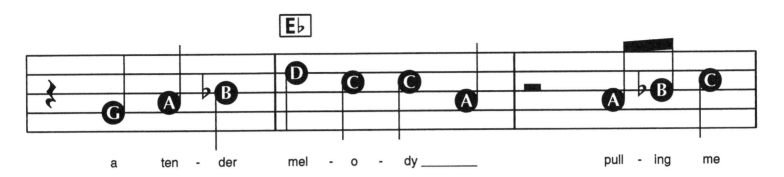
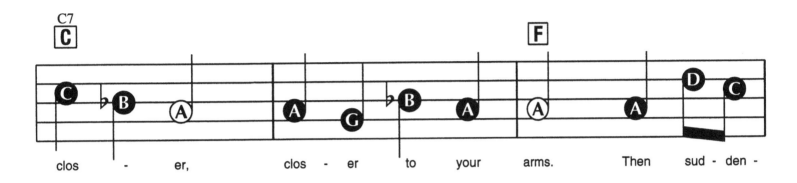
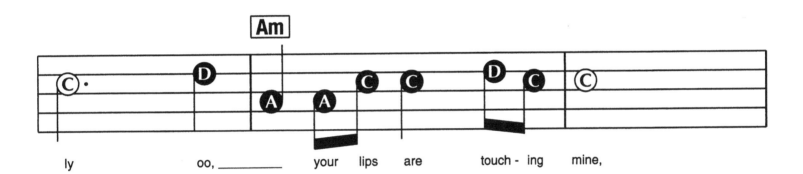
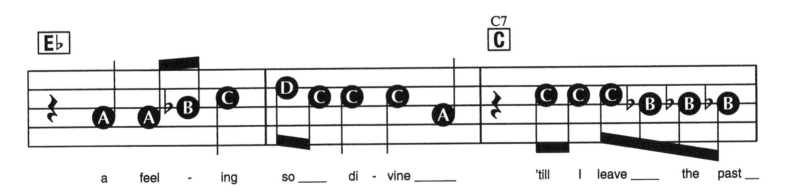
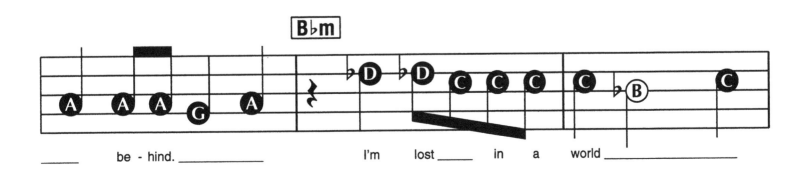

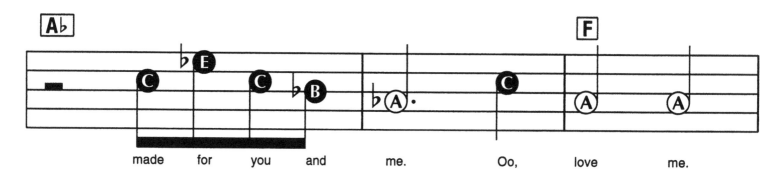

made for you and me. Oo, love me.

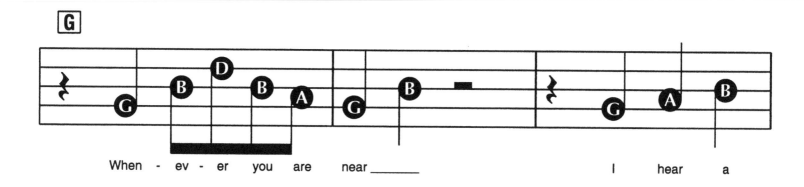

When - ev - er you are near _____ I hear a

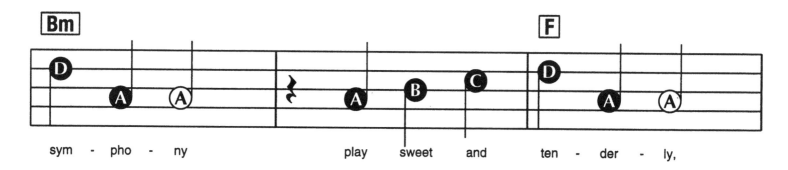

sym - pho - ny play sweet and ten - der - ly,

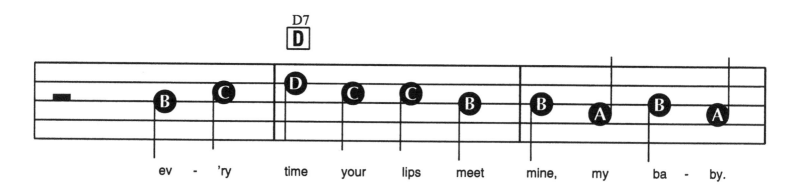

ev - 'ry time your lips meet mine, my ba - by.

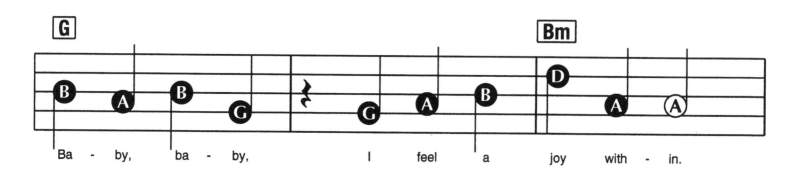

Ba - by, ba - by, I feel a joy with - in.

61

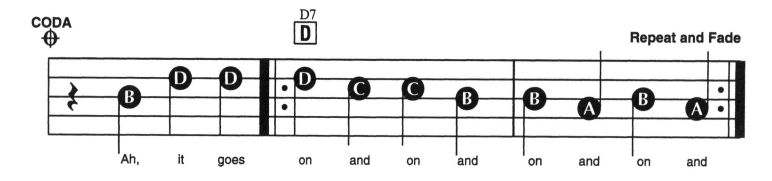

Additional Lyrics

2. Whenever you are near
   I hear a symphony,
   each time you speak to me
   I hear a tender rhapsody of love, love.

3. Baby, baby,
   as you stand up holding me
   whispering how much you care
   a thousand violins fill the air now.

4. Baby, baby,
   don't let this moment end.
   Keep standing close to me,
   oo so close to me, baby, baby.

I Will Follow Him
(I Will Follow You)

Registration 4
Rhythm: Rock or Pops

English Lyric by Norman Gimbel and Arthur Altman
Original Lyric by Jacques Plante
Music by J.W. Stole and Del Roma

I will fol - low him,_____ fol - low him wher - ev - er

he may go._____ There is - n't an o - cean too

deep, a moun - tain so high it can keep me a -

way._____ I must fol - low him,_____ ev - er since he touched my

hand I knew_____ that near him I al - ways must be, and

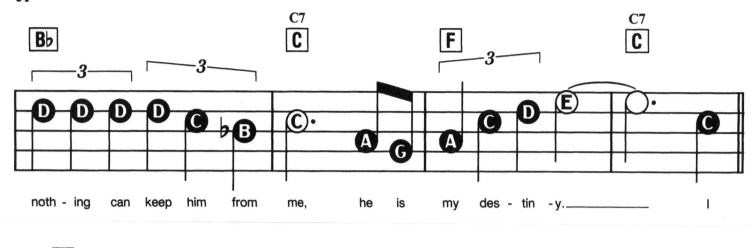

noth - ing can keep him from me, he is my des - tin -y._____ I

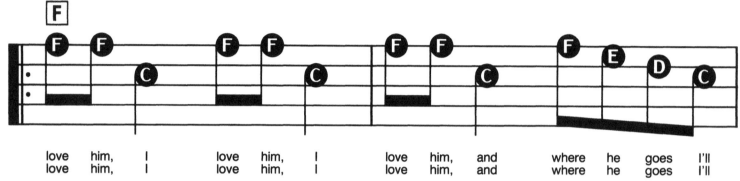

love him, I love him, I love him, and where he goes I'll
love him, I love him, I love him, and where he goes I'll

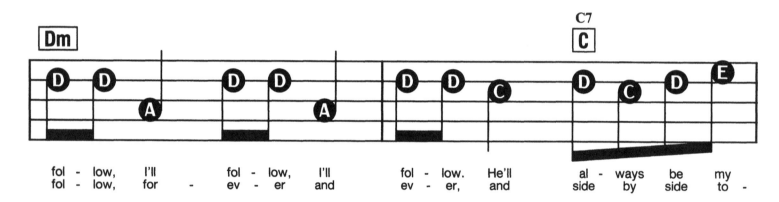

fol - low, I'll fol - low, I'll fol - low. He'll al - ways be my
fol - low, for - ev - er and ev - er, and side by side to -

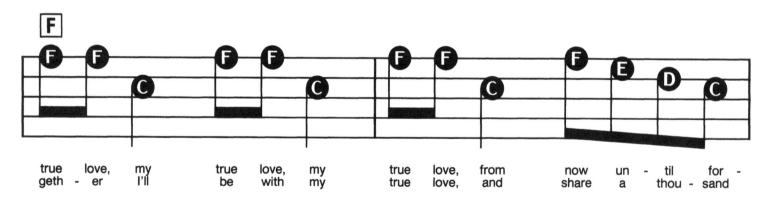

true love, my true love, my true love, from now un - til for -
geth - er I'll be with my true love, and share a thou - sand

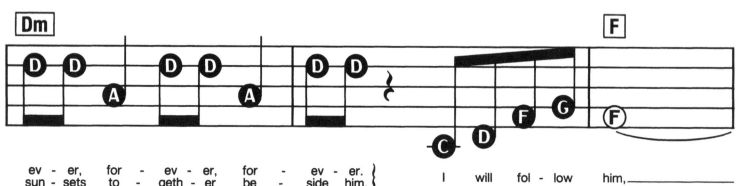

ev - er, for - ev - er, for - ev - er. I will fol - low him,_____
sun - sets to - geth - er be - side him.

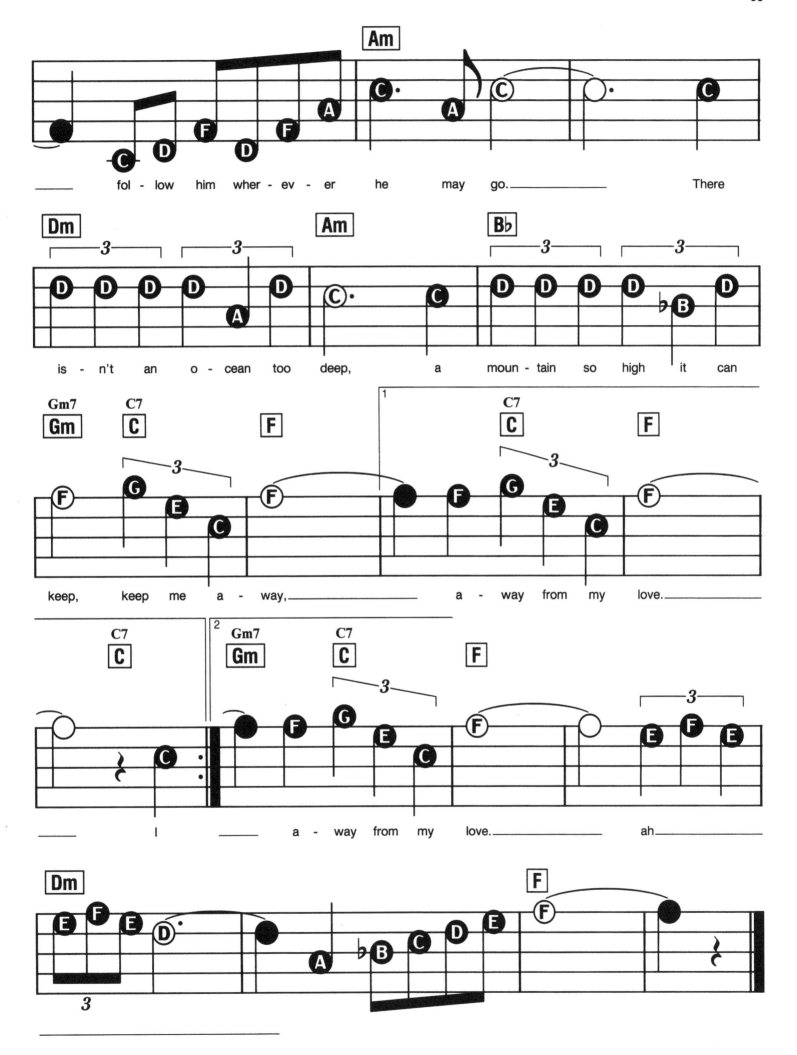

I Want to Hold Your Hand

Registration 3
Rhythm: Rock

Words and Music by John Lennon
and Paul McCartney

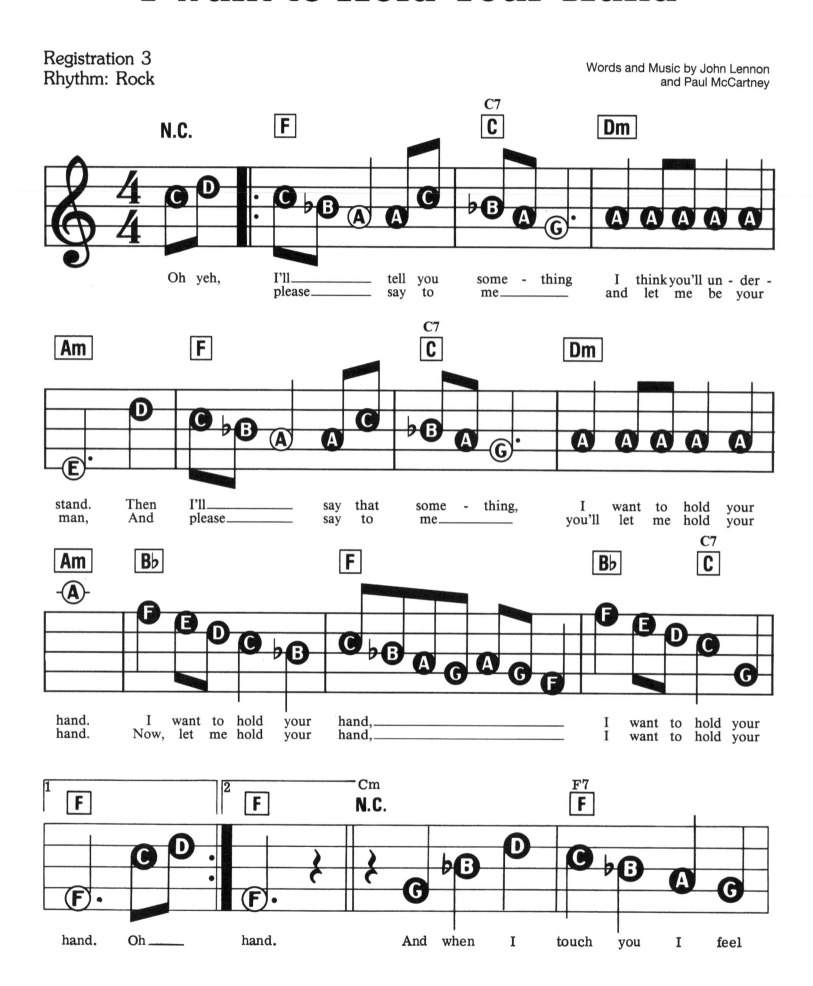

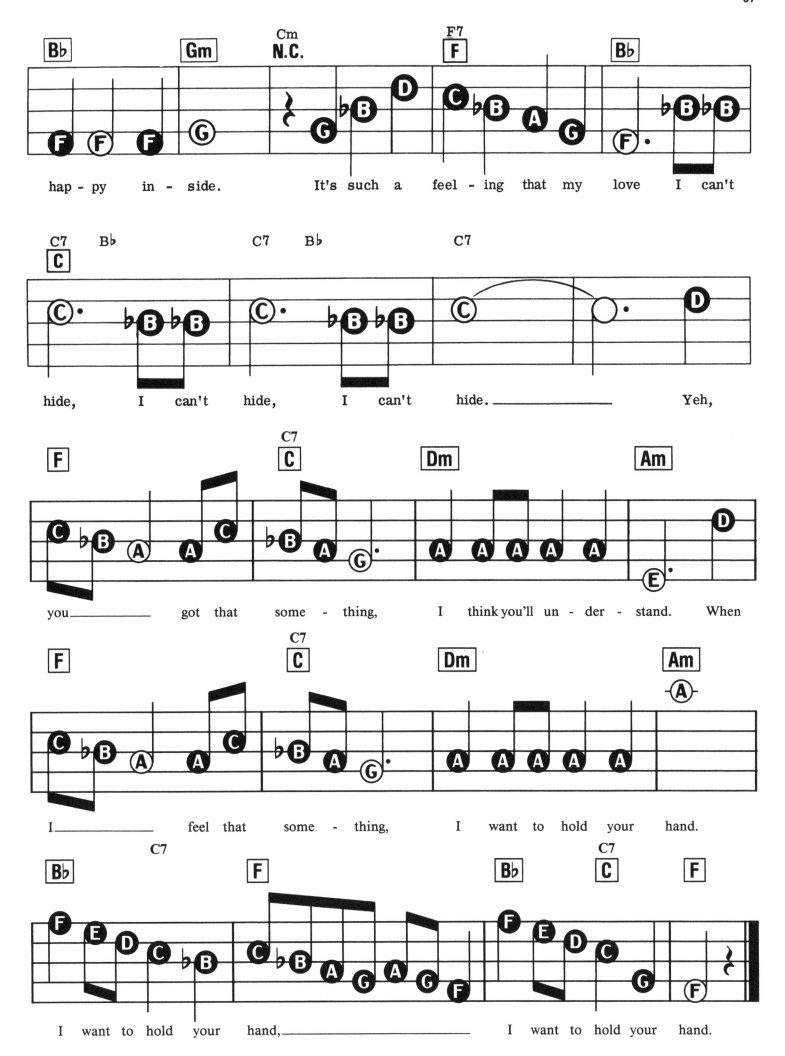

If I Were a Carpenter

Registration 3
Rhythm: Country

Words and Music by
Tim Hardin

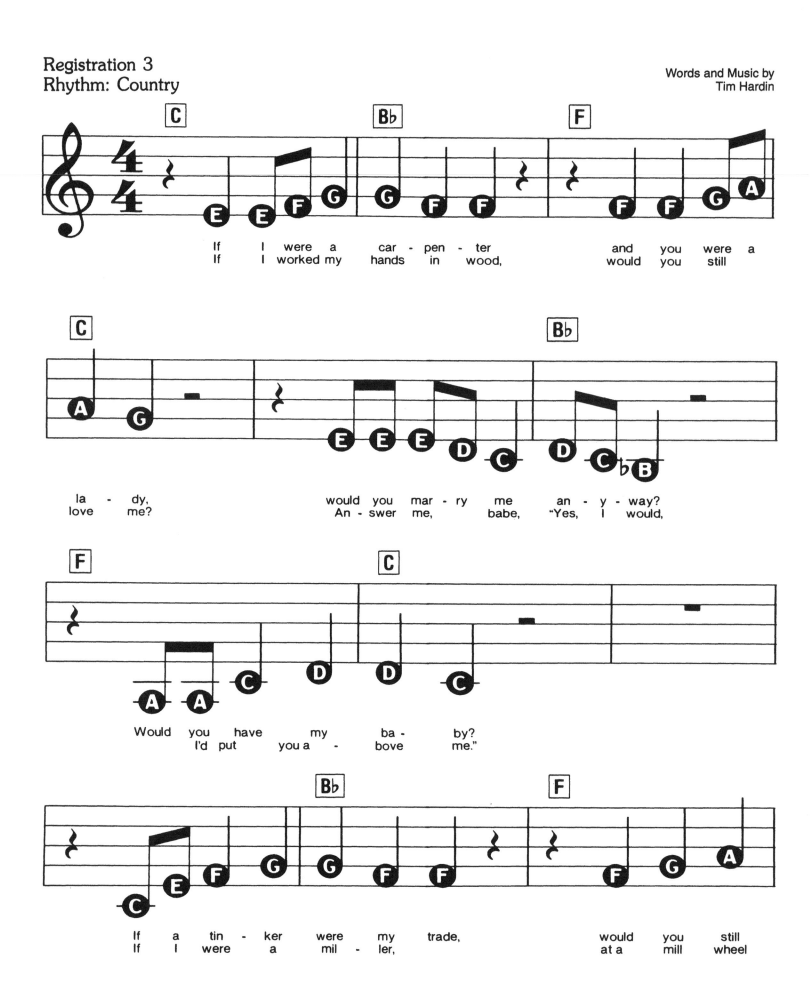

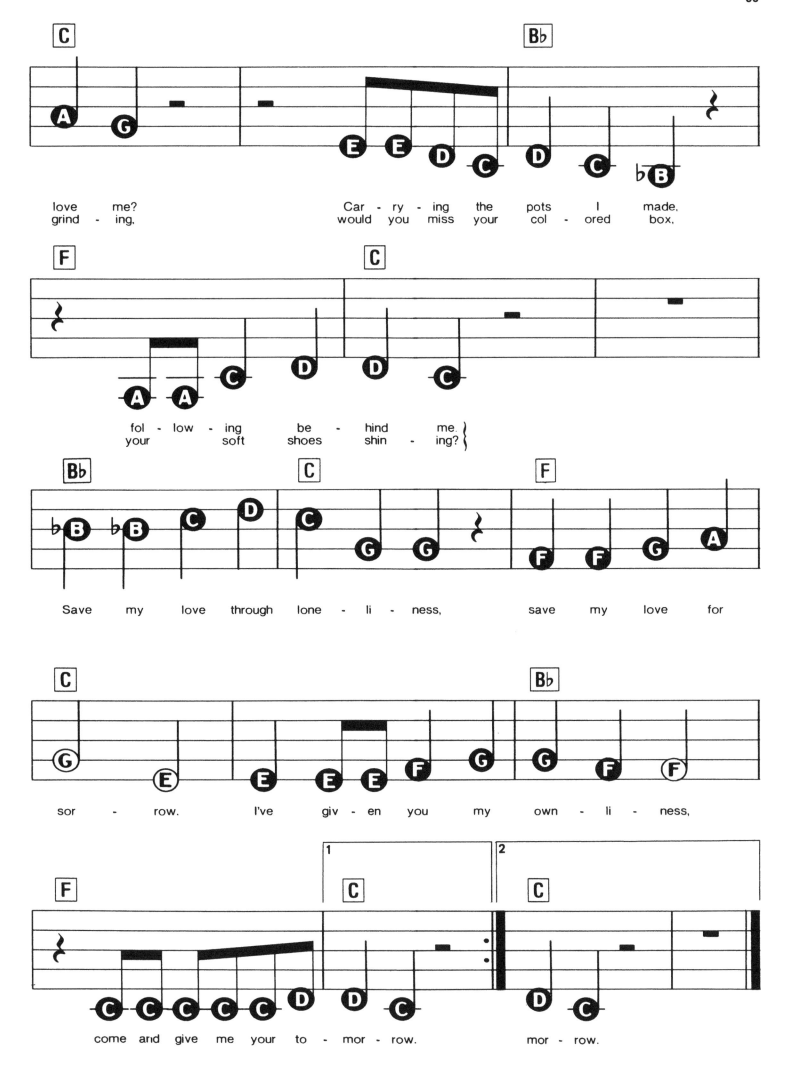

Let's Hang On

Registration 4
Rhythm: Rock or 8 Beat

Words and Music by Bob Crewe,
Sandy Linzer and Denny Randell

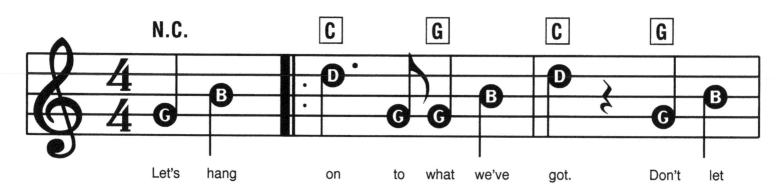

Let's hang on to what we've got. Don't let

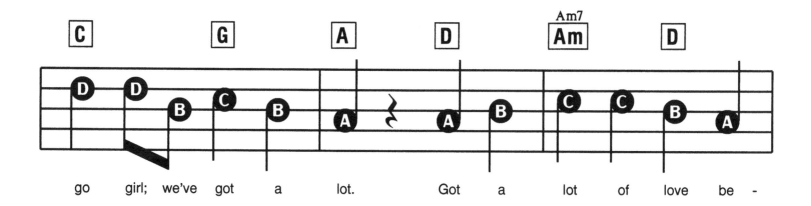

go girl; we've got a lot. Got a lot of love be -

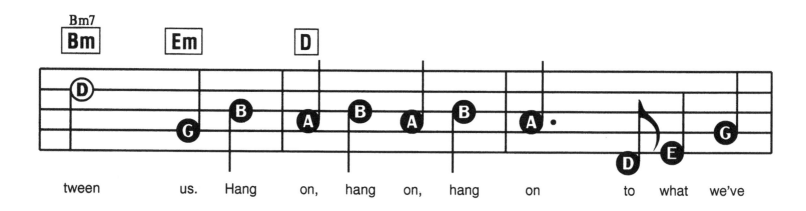

tween us. Hang on, hang on, hang on to what we've

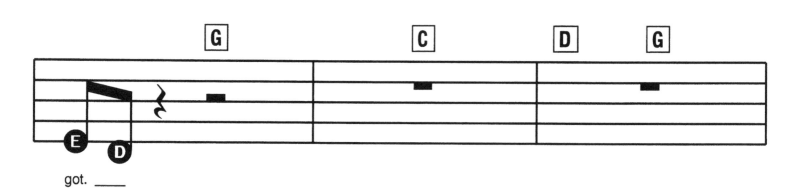

got. ____

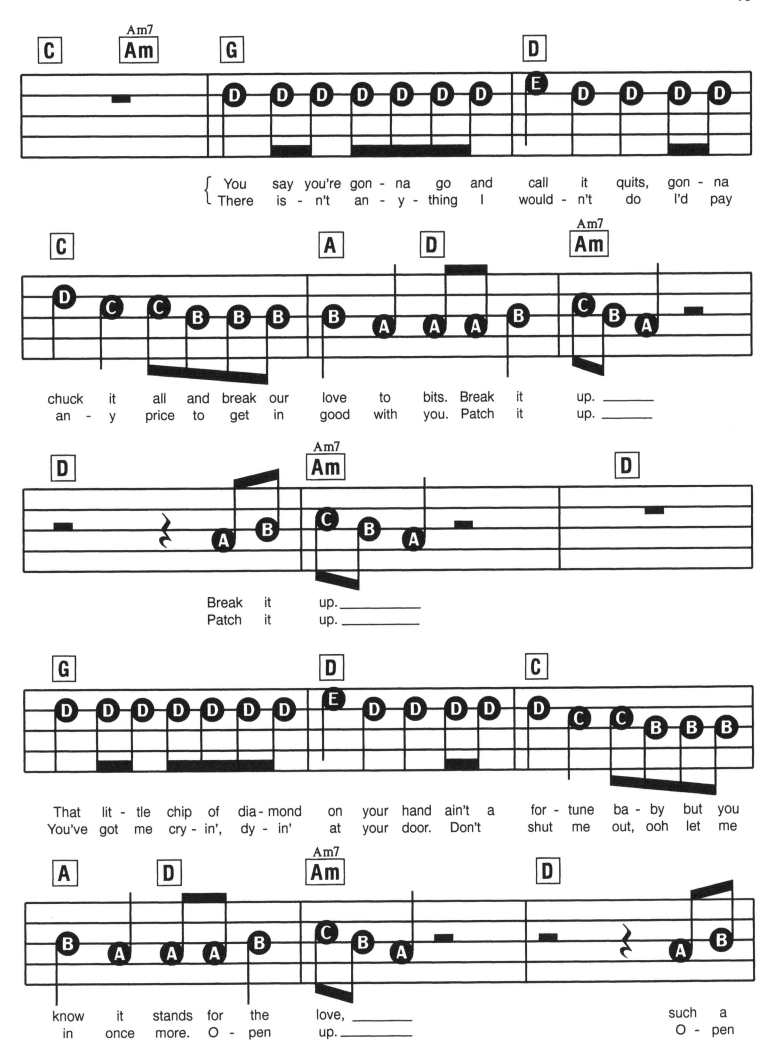

72

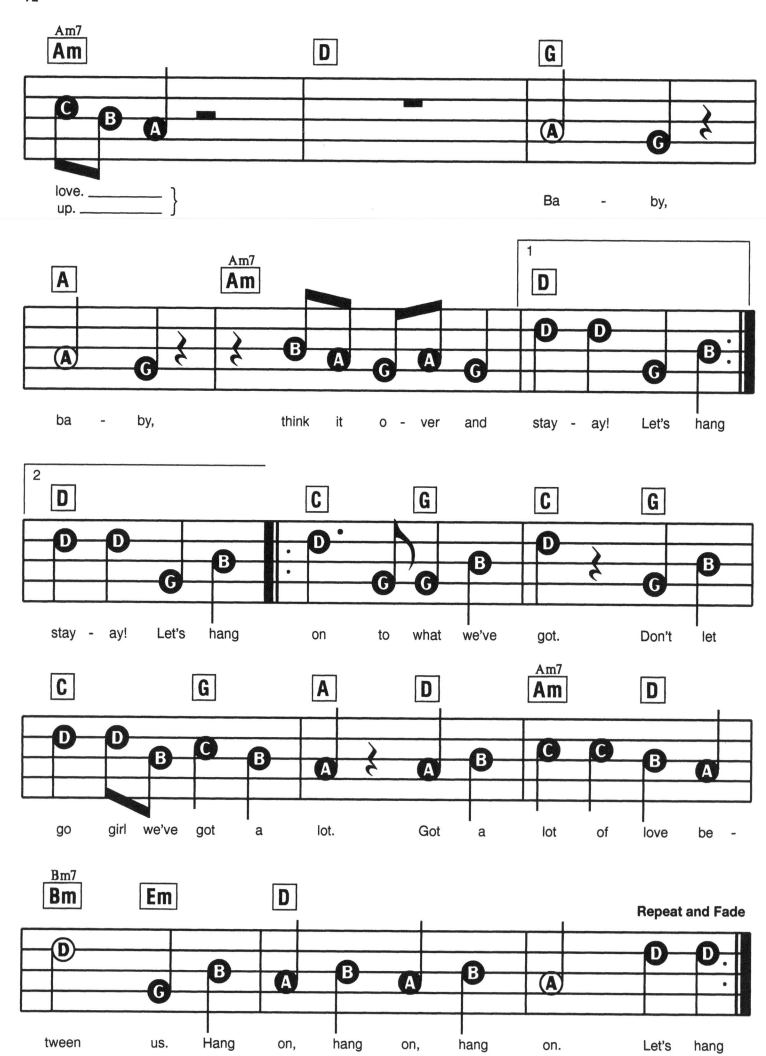

Love Potion Number 9

from SMOKEY JOE'S CAFE

Registration 9
Rhythm: Rock or Pop

Words and Music by Jerry Leiber
and Mike Stoller

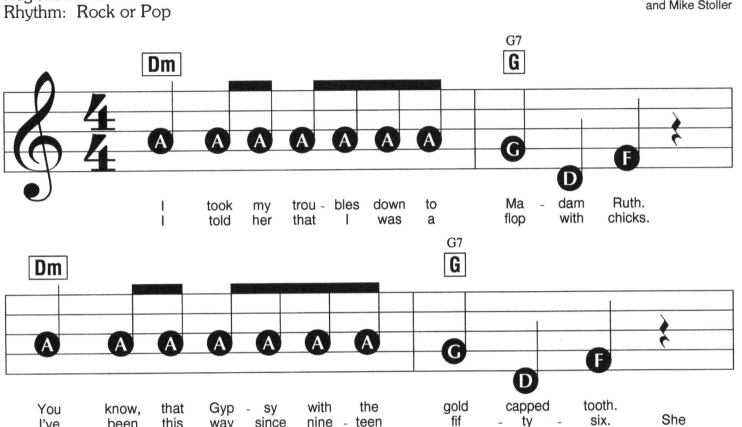

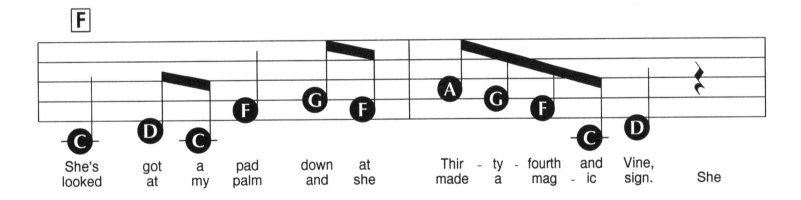

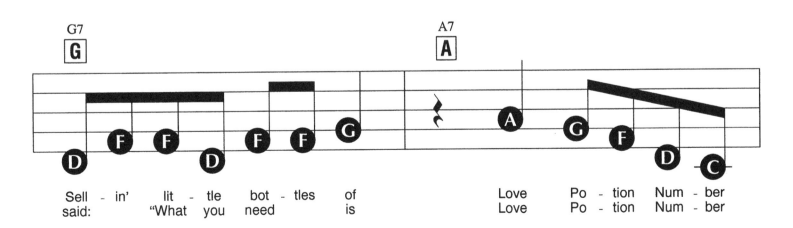

74

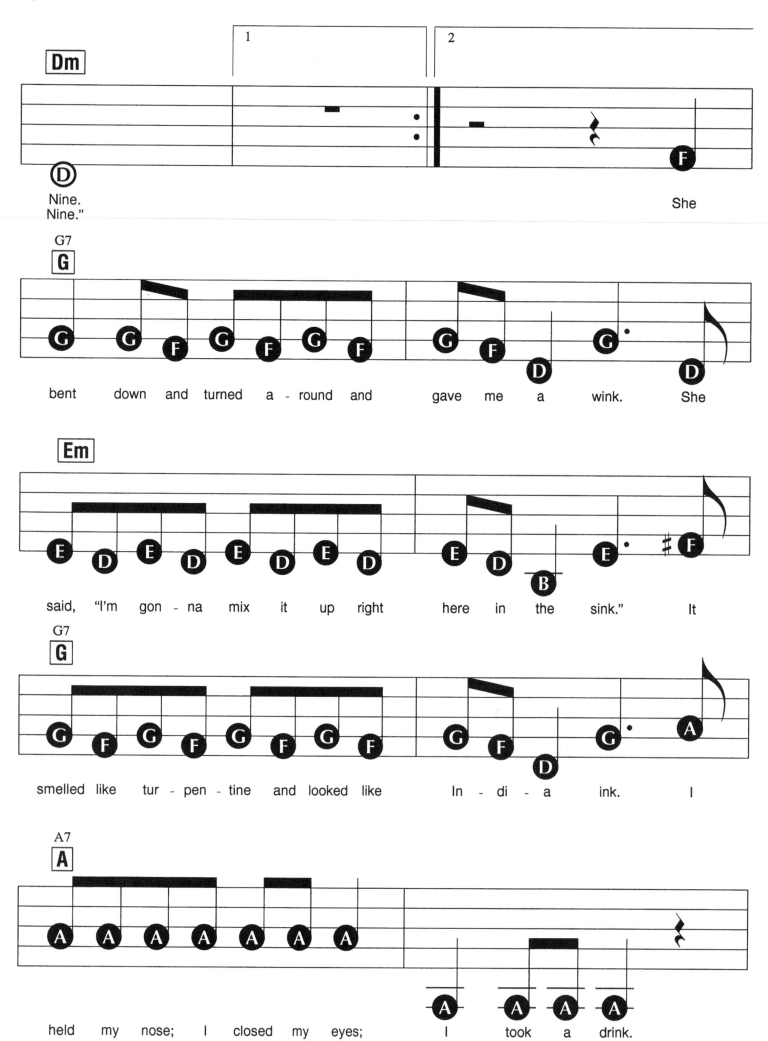

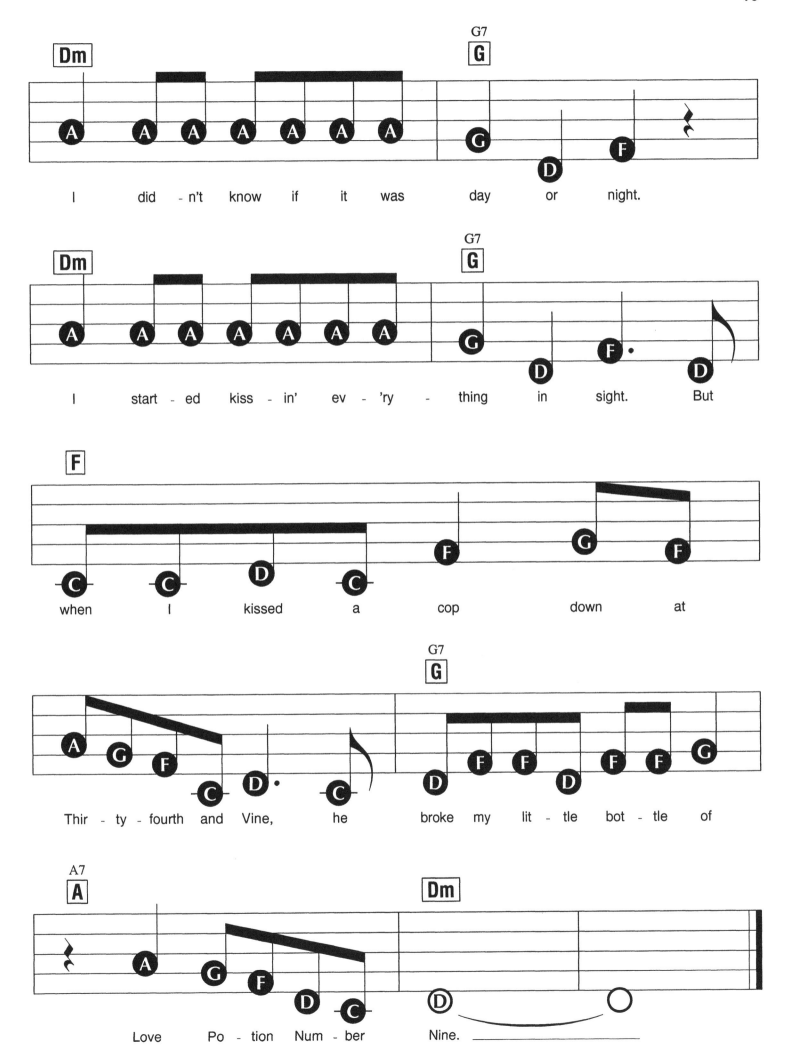

Let's Live for Today

Registration 1
Rhythm: Rock

Words and Music by Guido Cenciarelli,
Giulio Rapetti and Norman David

When I think of all the wor - ries peo - ple seem to
We were nev - er meant to wor - ry the way that peo - ple

find and how they're in a hur - ry to com - pli - cate their
do and I don't mean to hur - ry as long as I'm with

mind by chas - ing af - ter mon - ey and dreams that can't come
you. We'll take it nice and eas - y and use my sim - ple

true, I'm glad that we are dif - f'rent. We've bet - ter things to
plan. You'll be my lov - ing wom - an. I'll be your lov - ing

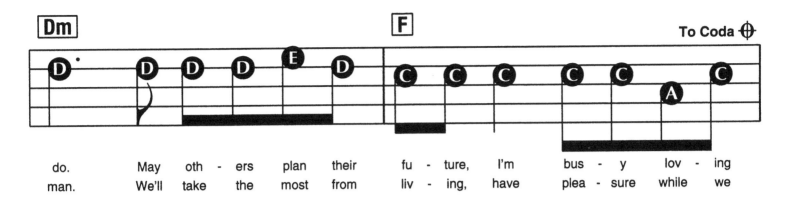

To Coda

do. May oth - ers plan their fu - ture, I'm bus - y lov - ing
man. We'll take the most from liv - ing, have plea - sure while we

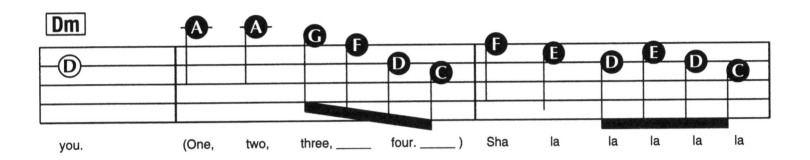

you. (One, two, three, _____ four. _____) Sha la la la la la

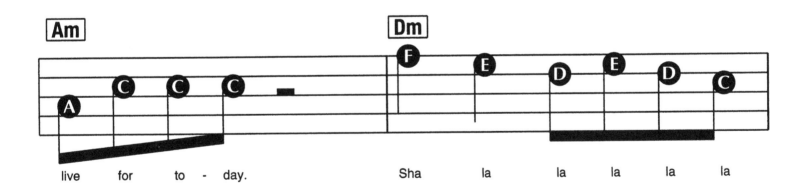

live for to - day. Sha la la la la la

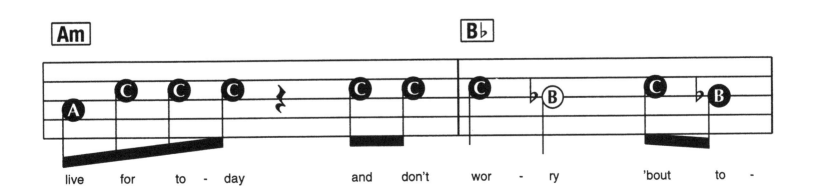

live for to - day and don't wor - ry 'bout to -

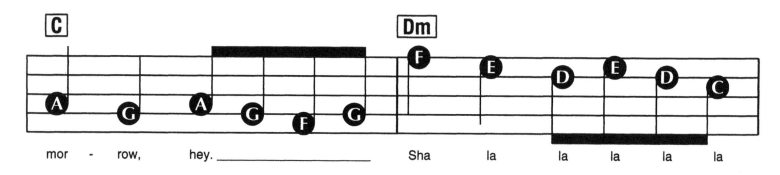

mor - row, hey. _____ Sha la la la la la

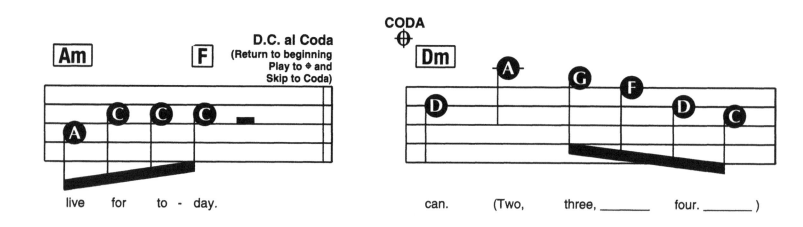

Am F

D.C. al Coda
(Return to beginning
Play to ⊕ and
Skip to Coda)

live for to - day.

CODA

Dm

can. (Two, three, _____ four. _____)

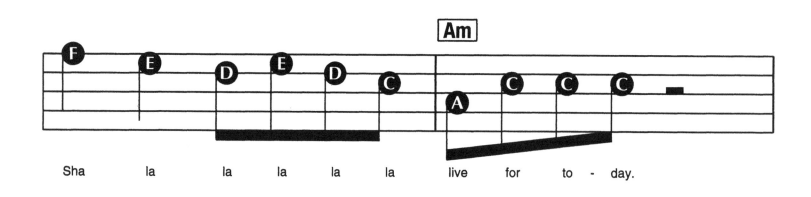

Sha la la la la la live for to - day.

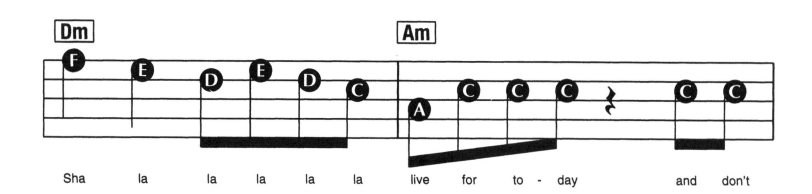

Sha la la la la la live for to - day and don't

79

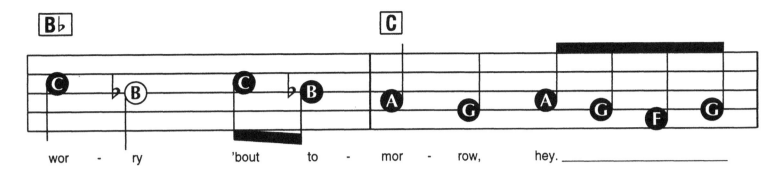

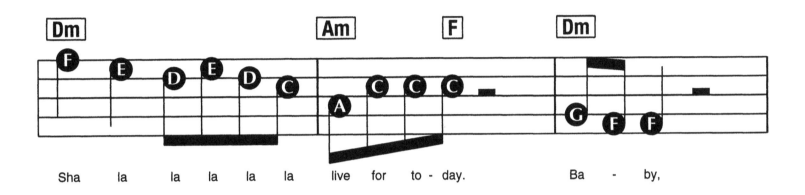

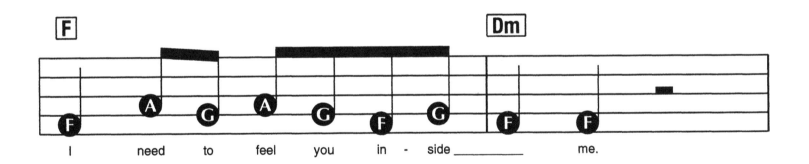

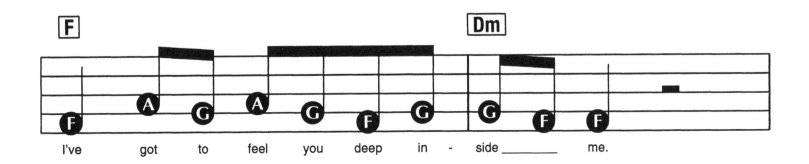

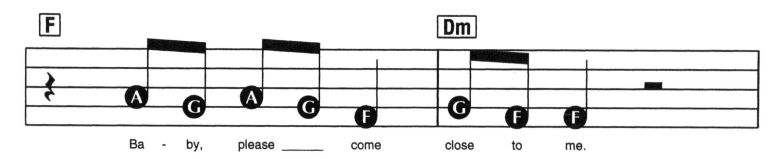

Ba - by, please _____ come close to me.

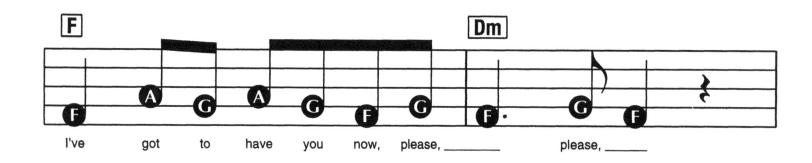

I've got to have you now, please, _____ please, _____

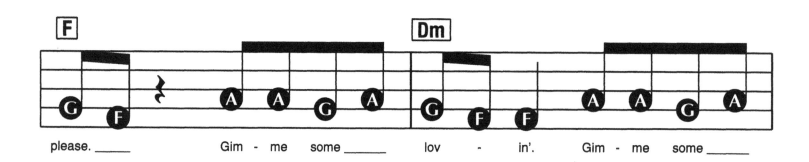

please. _____ Gim - me some _____ lov - in'. Gim - me some _____

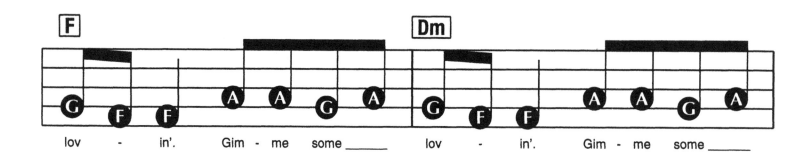

lov - in'. Gim - me some _____ lov - in'. Gim - me some _____

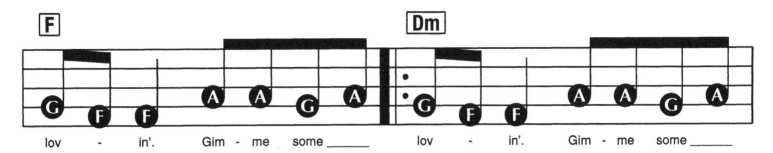

lov - in'. Gim - me some _____ lov - in'. Gim - me some _____

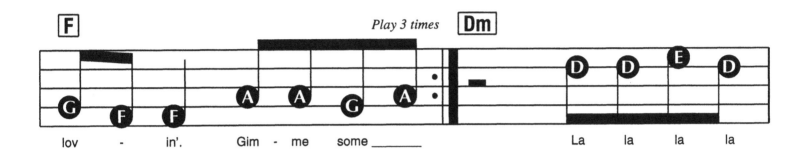

lov - in'. Gim - me some _____ La la la la

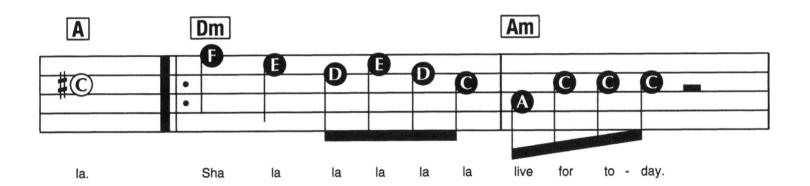

la. Sha la la la la la live for to - day.

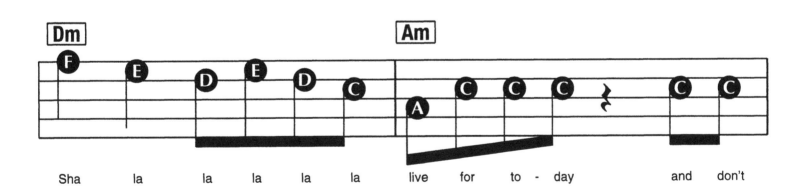

Sha la la la la la live for to - day and don't

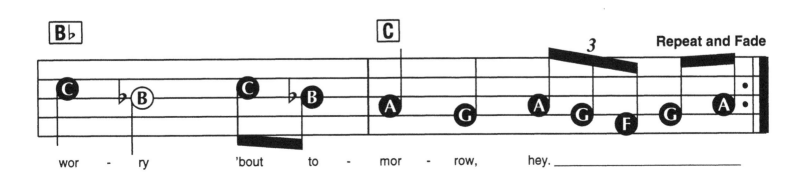

wor - ry 'bout to - mor - row, hey. _____

Love Me Do

Registration 4
Rhythm: Rock

Words and Music by John Lennon
and Paul McCartney

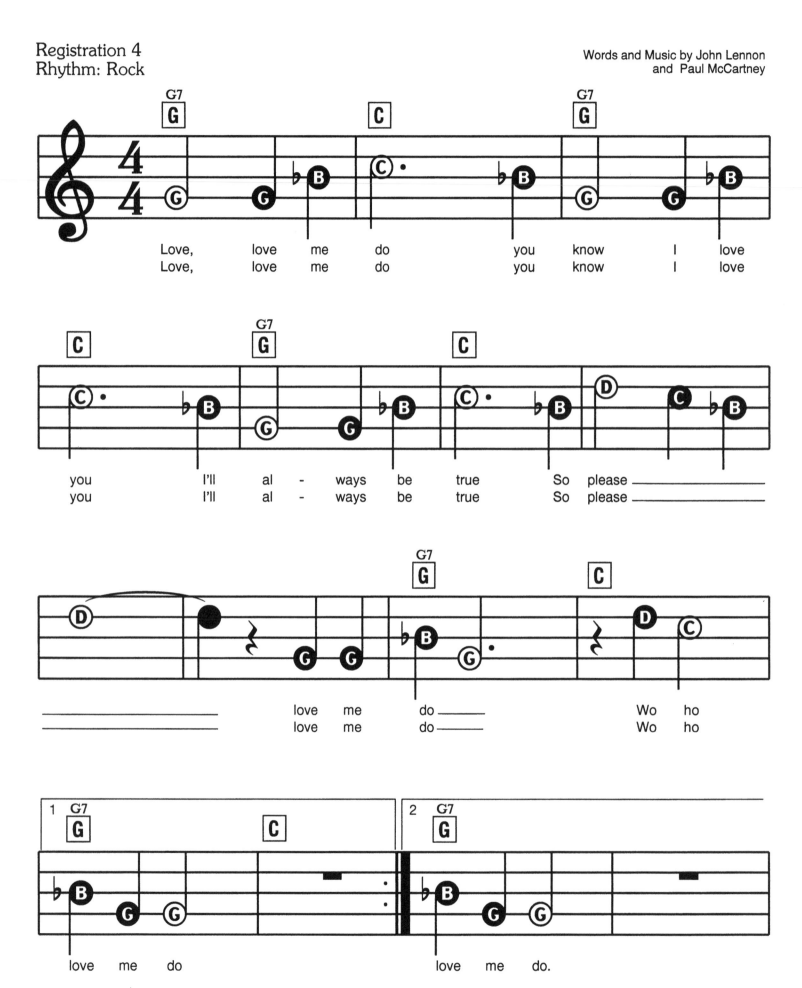

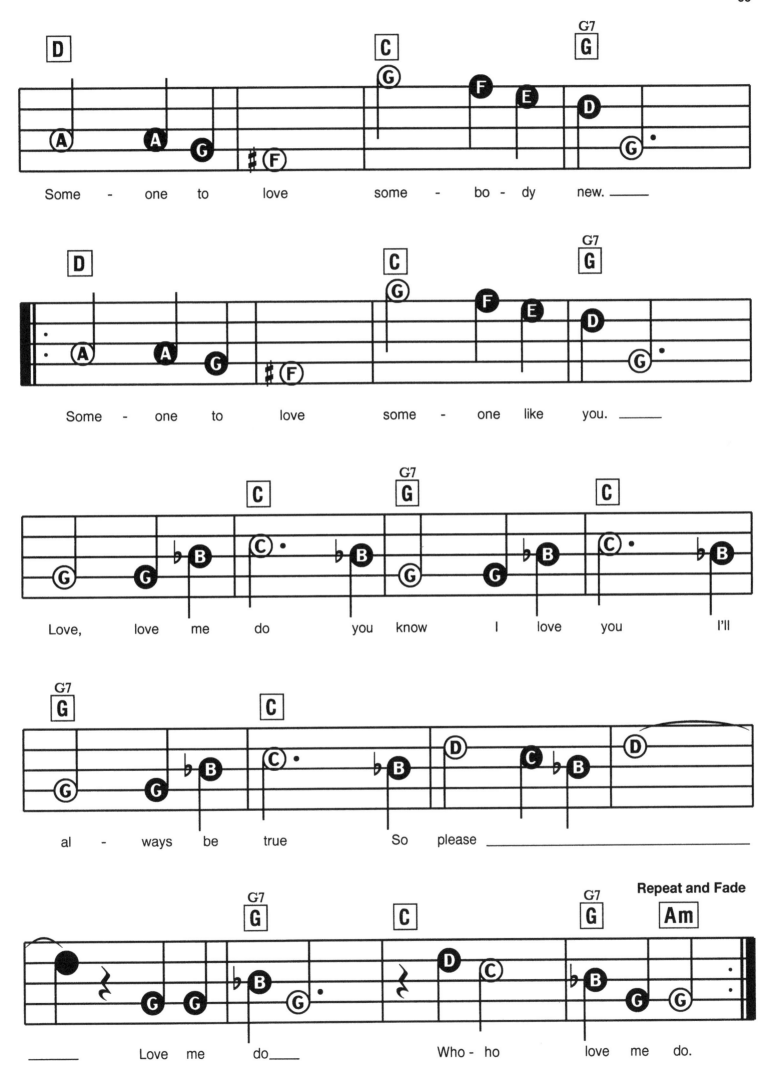

A Lover's Concerto

Registration 2
Rhythm: Rock or Slow Rock

Words and Music by Sandy Linzer
and Denny Randell

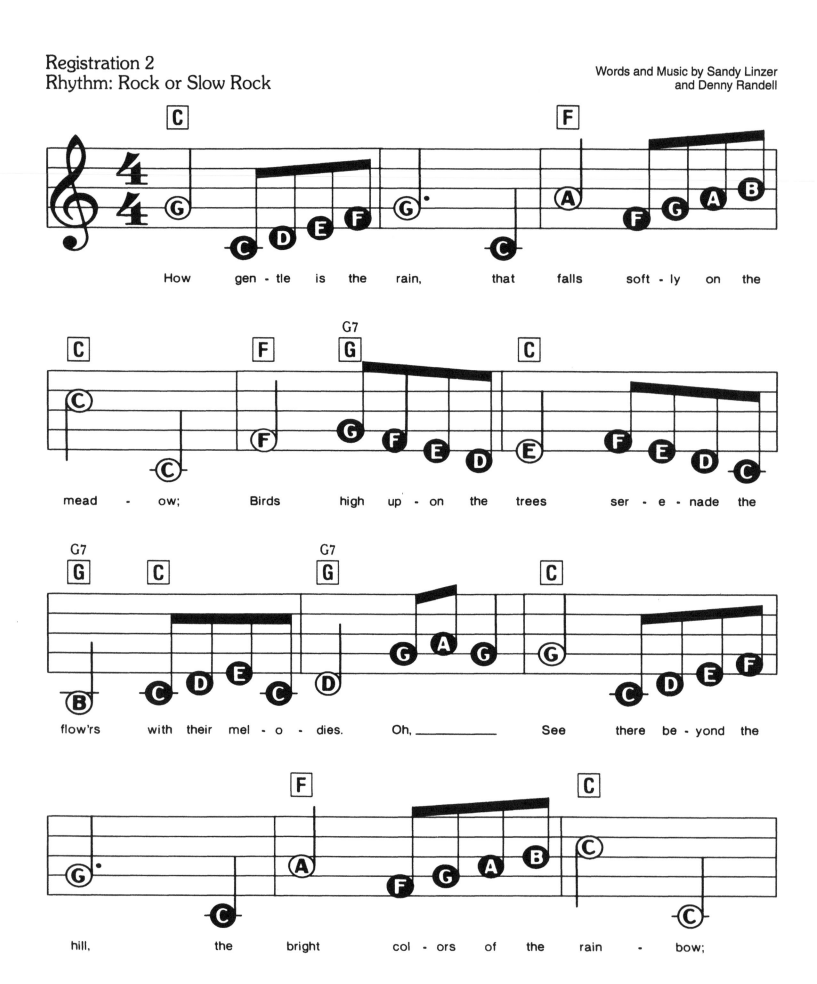

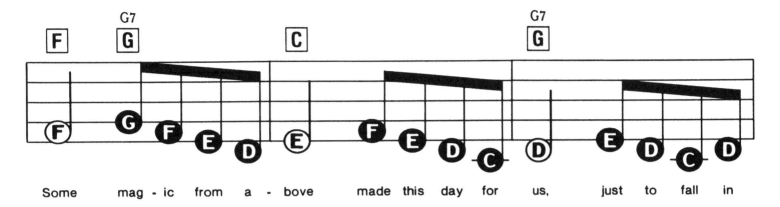

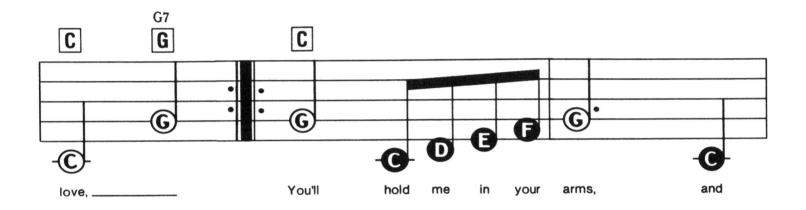

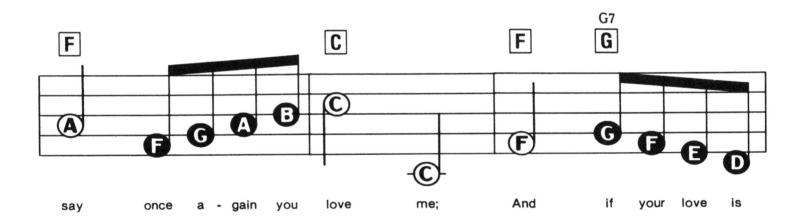

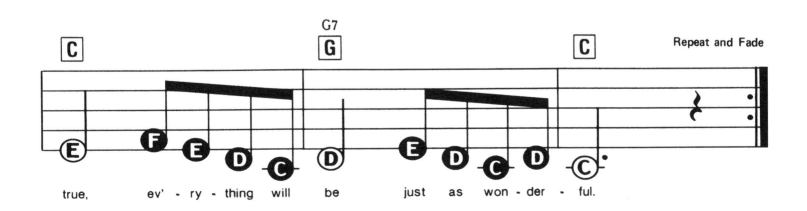

Memories

Registration 2
Rhythm: Rock

Words and Music by Billy Strange
and Scott Davis

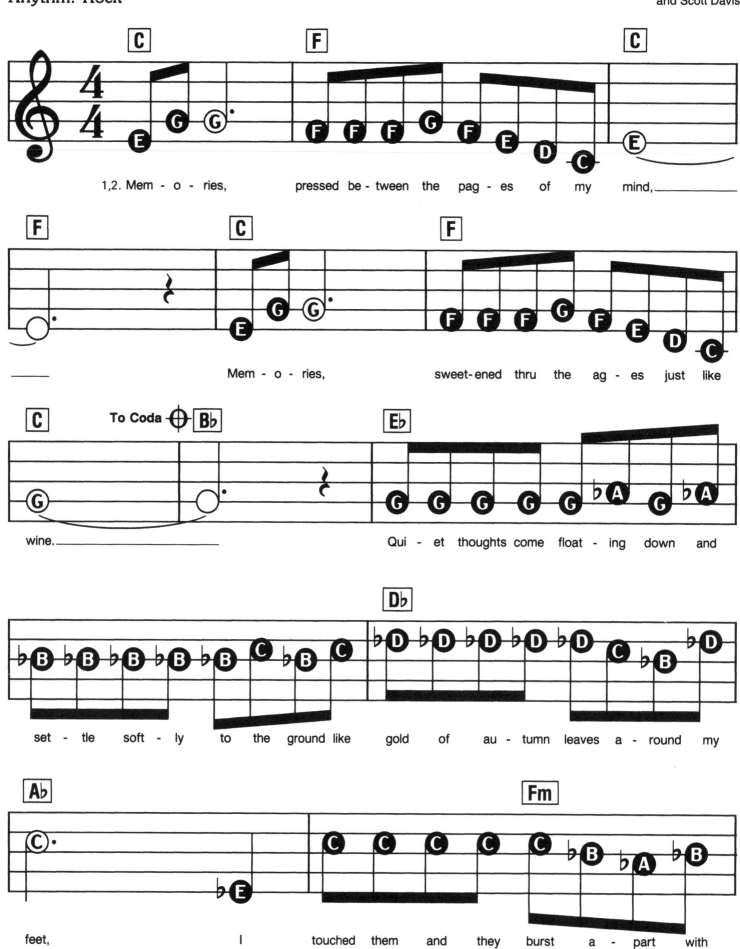

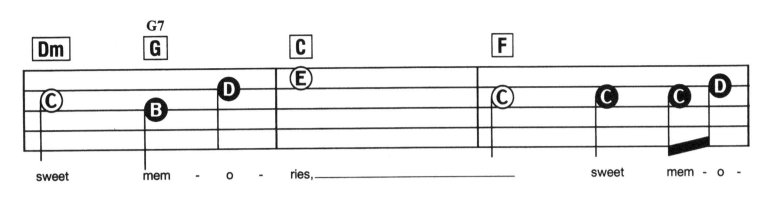

sweet mem - o - ries,_____ sweet mem - o -

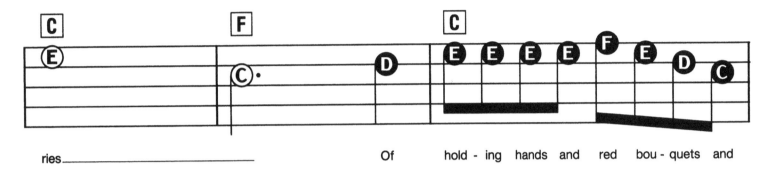

ries_____ Of hold - ing hands and red bou - quets and

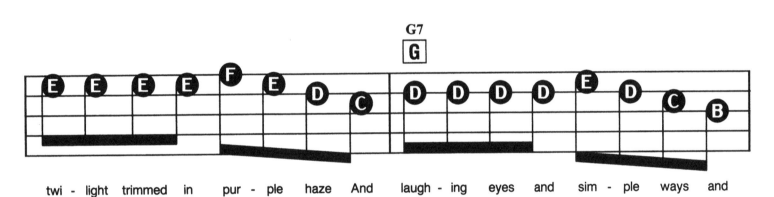

twi - light trimmed in pur - ple haze And laugh - ing eyes and sim - ple ways and

D.C. al Coda
(Return to beginning
Play to ⊕ and
skip to Coda)

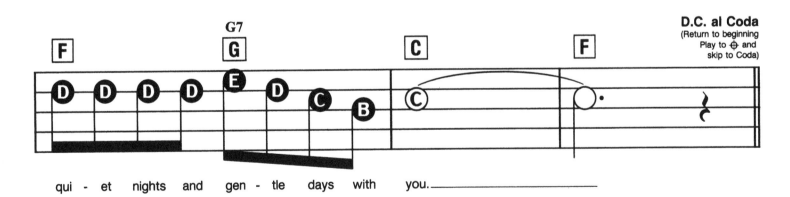

qui - et nights and gen - tle days with you._____

CODA

Repeat and Fade

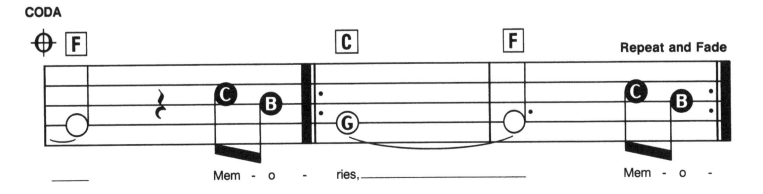

_____ Mem - o - ries,_____ Mem - o -

Monday, Monday

Registration 4
Rhythm: Rock

Words and Music by
John Phillips

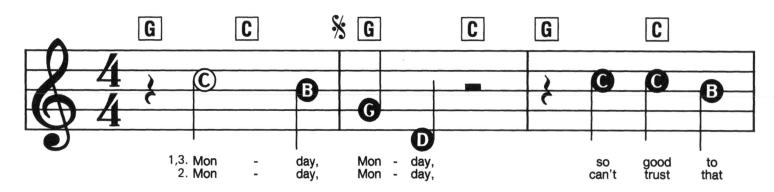

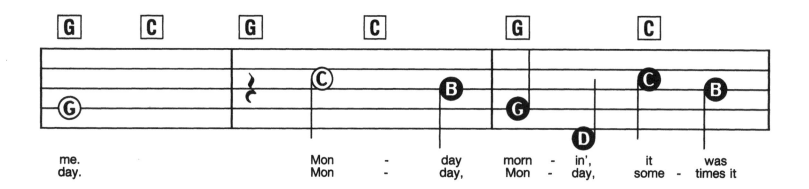

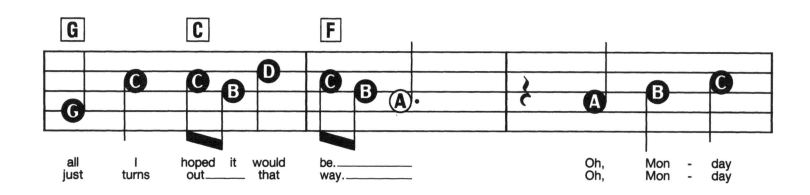

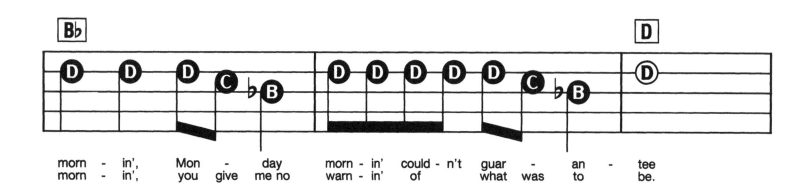

89

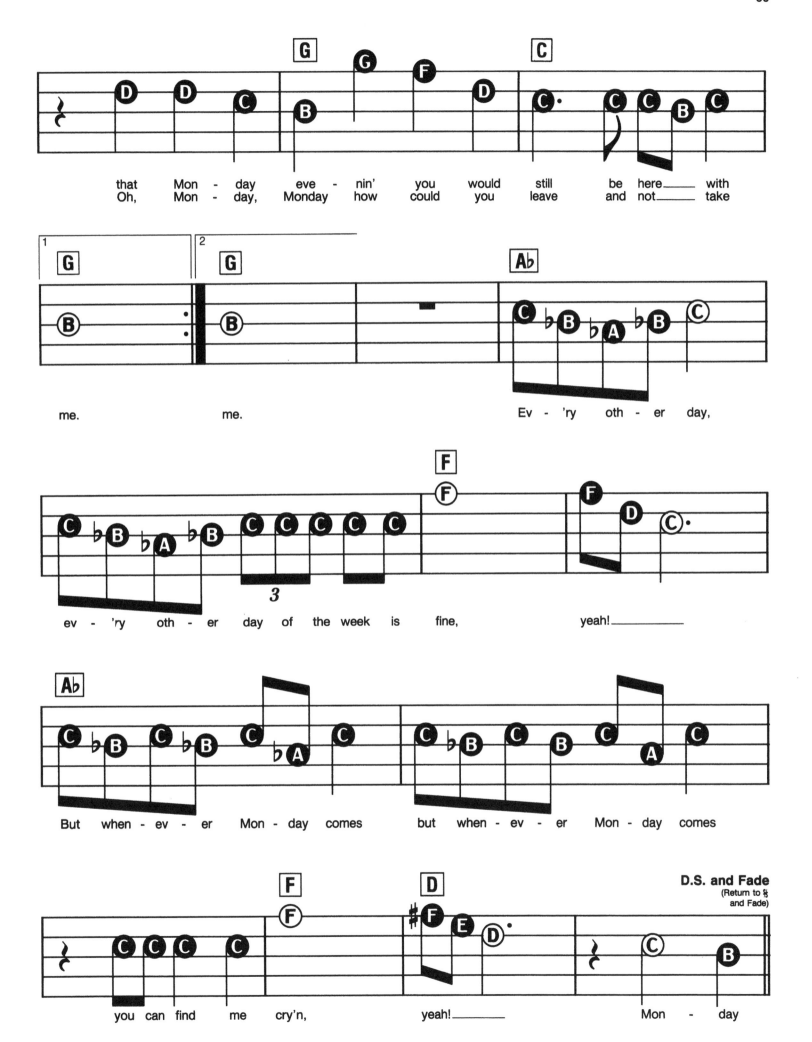

Money
(That's What I Want)

Registration 5
Rhythm: Rock 'n' Roll

Words and Music by Berry Gordy
and Janie Bradford

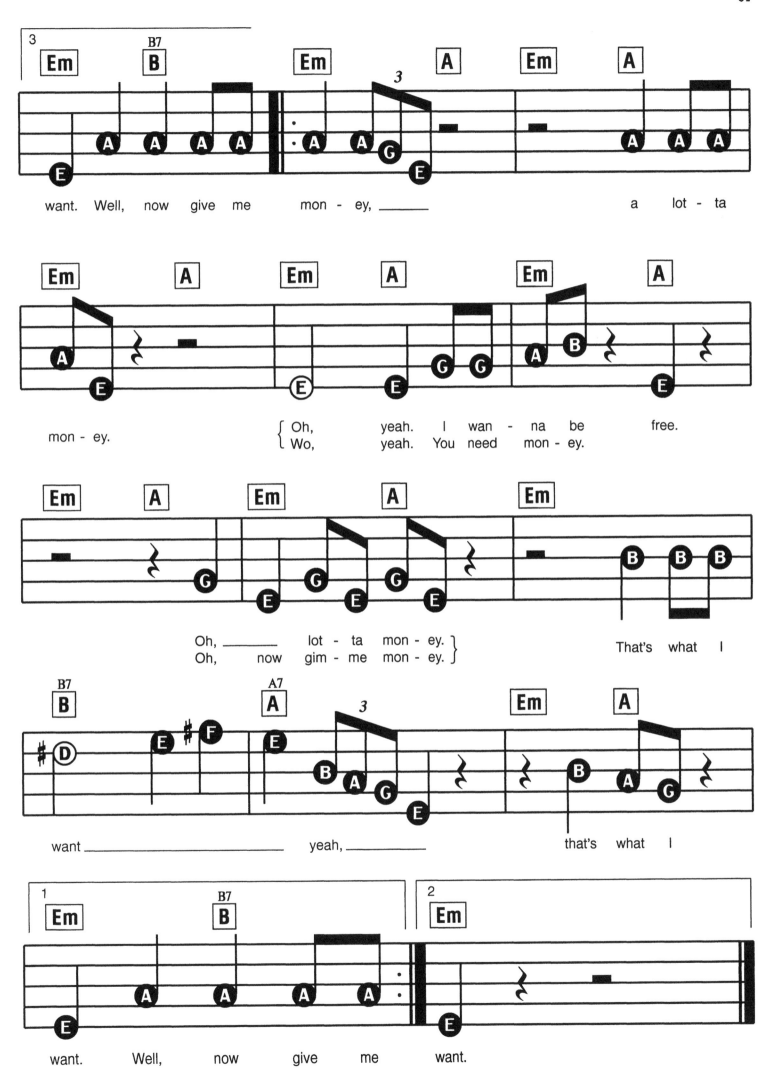

My Girl

Registration 9
Rhythm: Rock or 8 Beat

Words and Music by William "Smokey" Robinson
and Ronald White

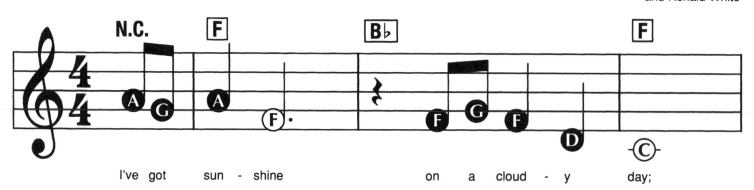

I've got sun - shine on a cloud - y day;

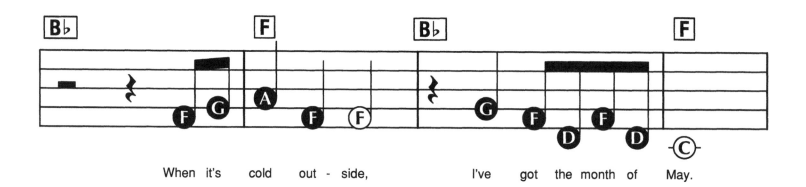

When it's cold out - side, I've got the month of May.

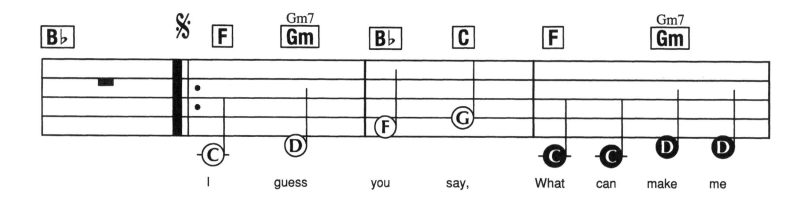

I guess you say, What can make me

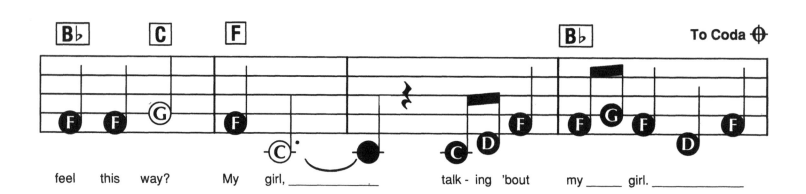

feel this way? My girl, _____ talk - ing 'bout my _____ girl. _____

93

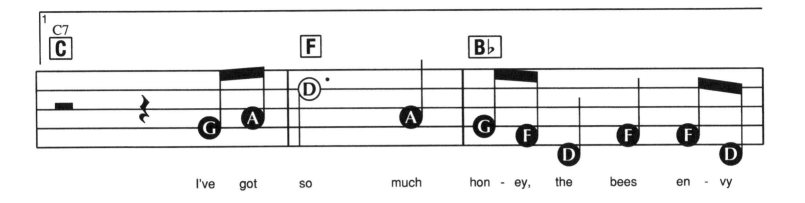

I've got so much hon - ey, the bees en - vy

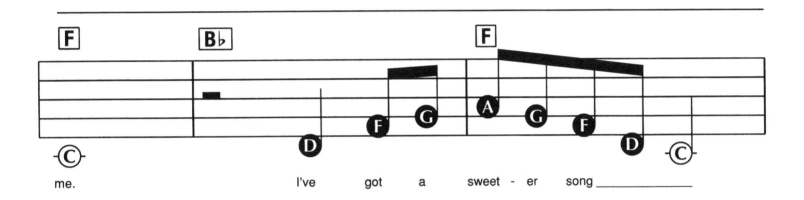

me. I've got a sweet - er song

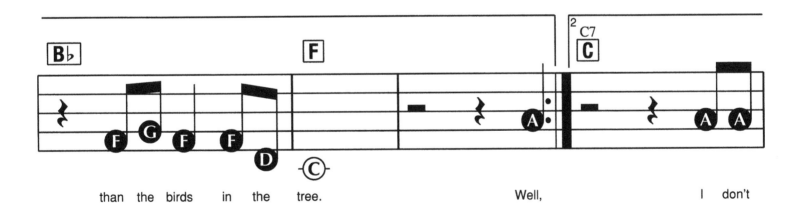

than the birds in the tree. Well, I don't

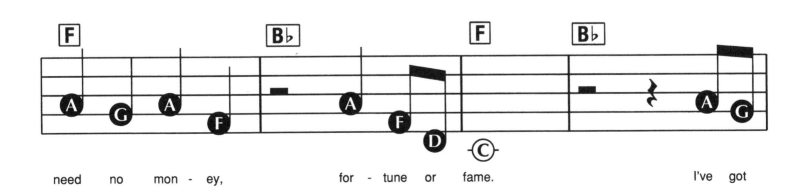

need no mon - ey, for - tune or fame. I've got

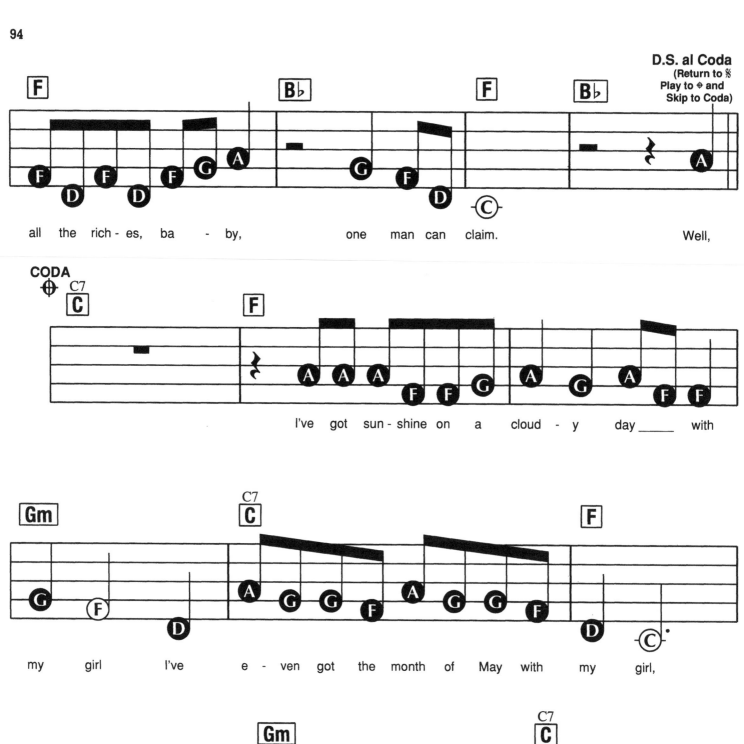

D.S. al Coda
(Return to %
Play to ⊕ and
Skip to Coda)

all the rich - es, ba - by, one man can claim. Well,

CODA

C7

I've got sun - shine on a cloud - y day _____ with

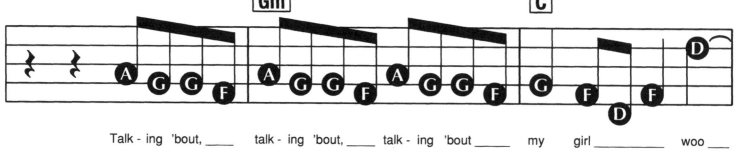

my girl I've e - ven got the month of May with my girl,

Talk - ing 'bout, ____ talk - ing 'bout, ____ talk - ing 'bout ____ my girl _____ woo ___

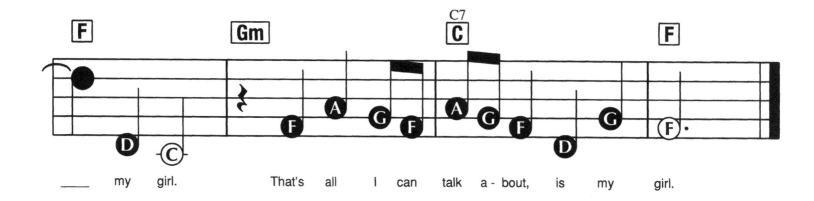

____ my girl. That's all I can talk a - bout, is my girl.

Oh, Pretty Woman

Registration 3
Rhythm: Rock or 8 Beat

Words and Music by Roy Orbison
and Bill Dees

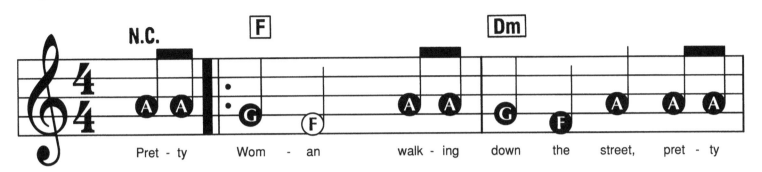

Pret - ty   Wom - an   walk - ing   down   the   street,   pret - ty

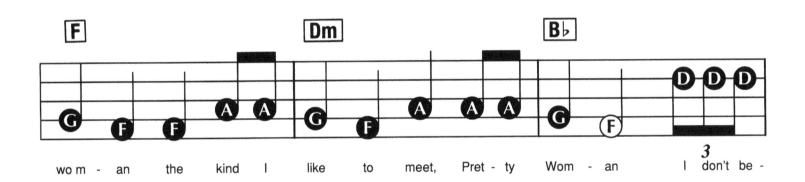

wo m - an   the   kind   I   like   to   meet,   Pret - ty   Wom - an   I   don't be -

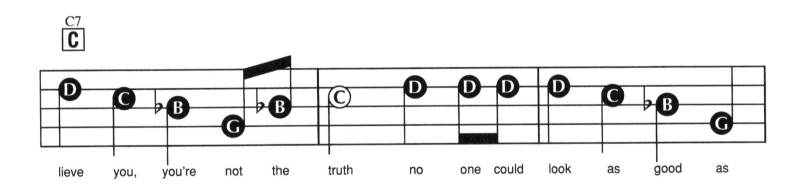

lieve   you,   you're   not   the   truth   no   one   could   look   as   good   as

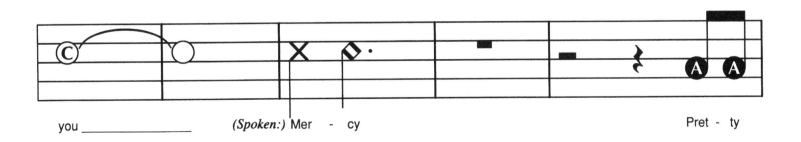

you _____   (Spoken:) Mer - cy   Pret - ty

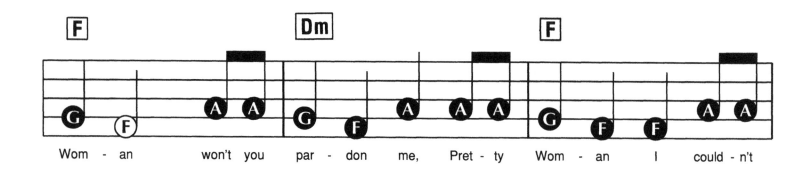

Wom - an won't you par - don me, Pret - ty Wom - an I could - n't

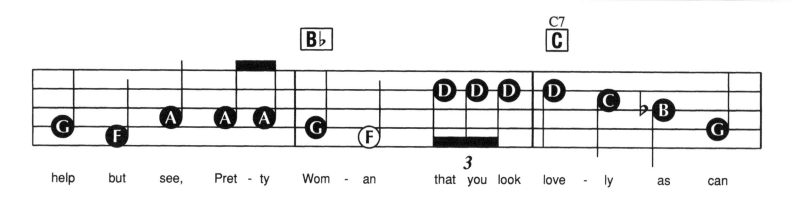

help but see, Pret - ty Wom - an that you look love - ly as can

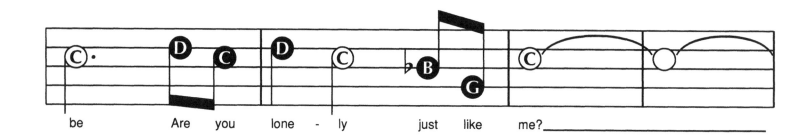

be Are you lone - ly just like me?_____

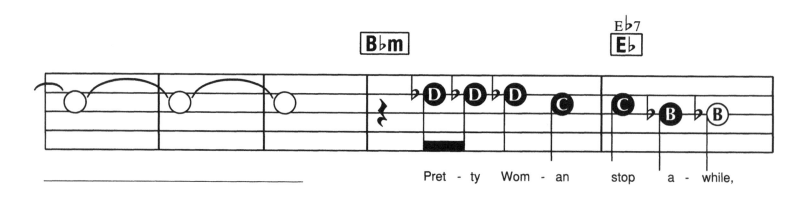

_____ Pret - ty Wom - an stop a - while,

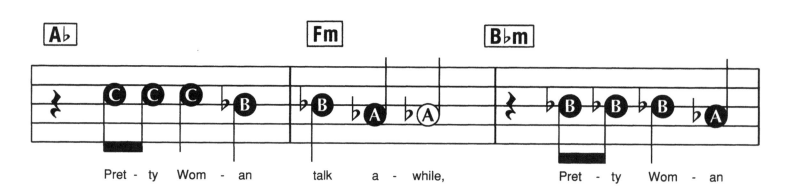

Pret - ty Wom - an talk a - while, Pret - ty Wom - an

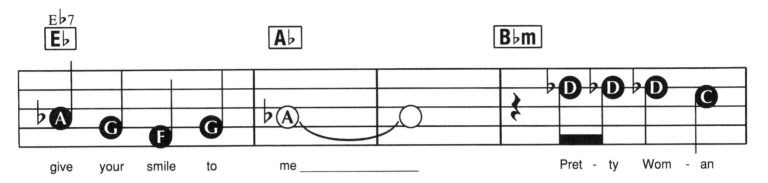

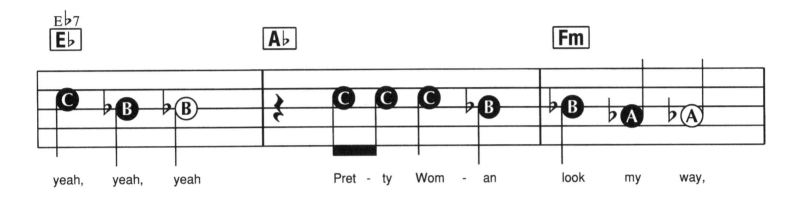

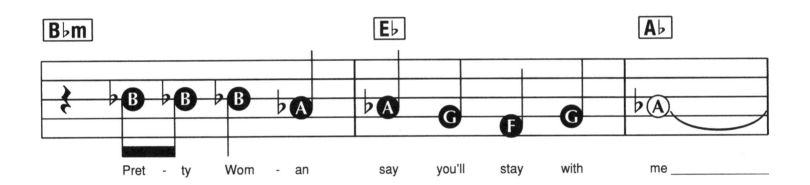

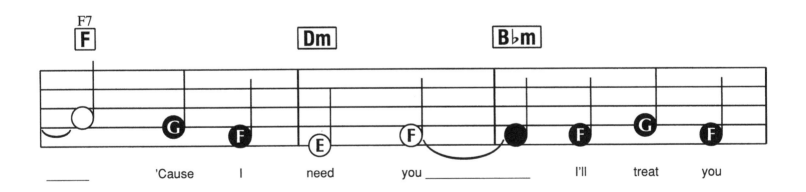

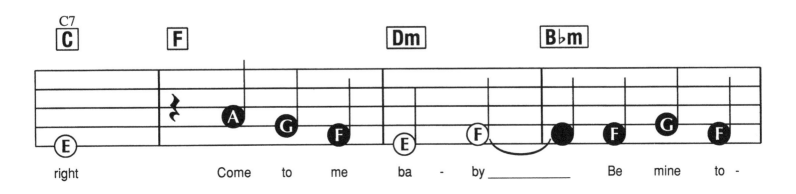

98

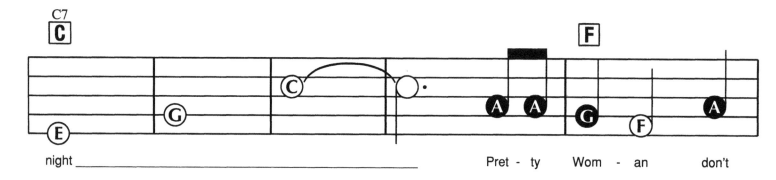

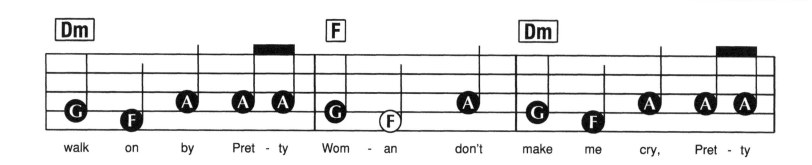

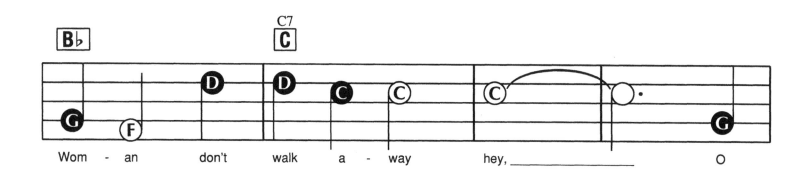

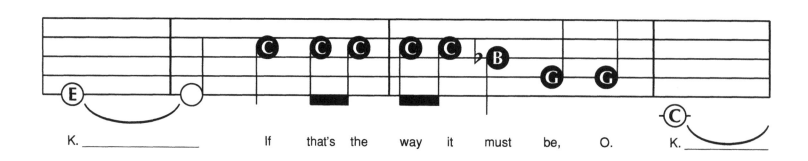

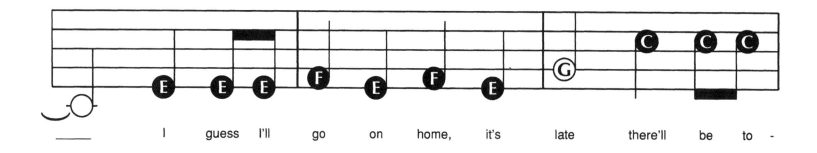

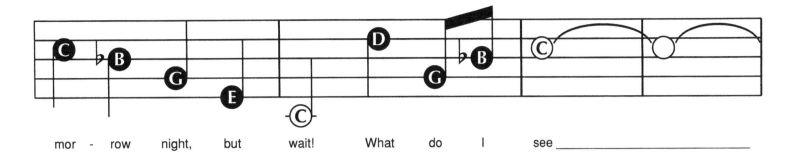

mor - row night, but wait! What do I see _____

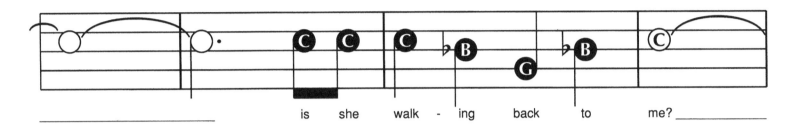

_____ is she walk - ing back to me? _____

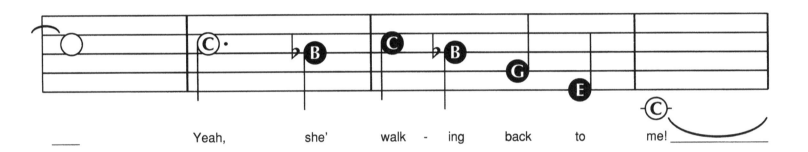

___ Yeah, she' walk - ing back to me! _____

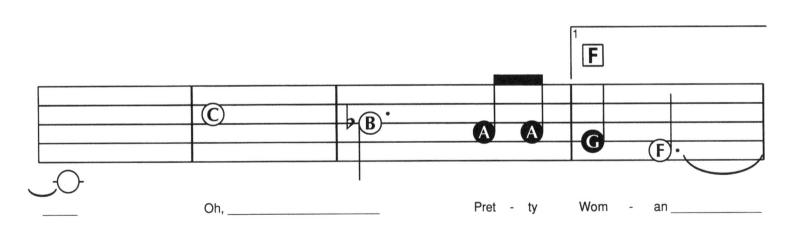

___ Oh, _____ Pret - ty Wom - an _____

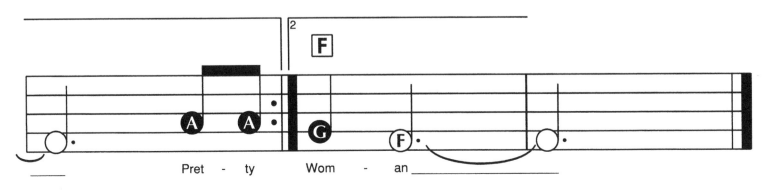

___ Pret - ty Wom - an _____

(You Make Me Feel Like)
A Natural Woman

Registration 7
Rhythm: Waltz or Slow Rock

Words and Music by Gerry Goffin,
Carole King and Jerry Wexler

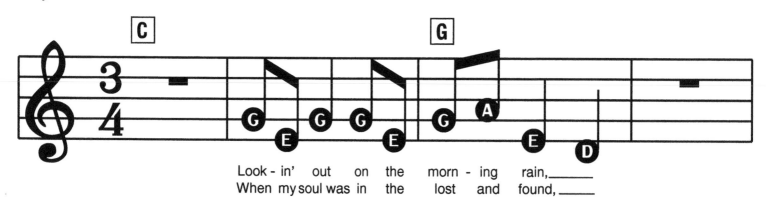

Look - in' out on the morn - ing rain,_____
When my soul was in the lost and found, _____

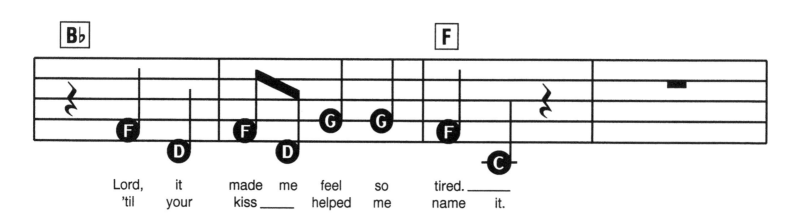

I used to feel un - in - spired. _____
you came a - long to claim it.

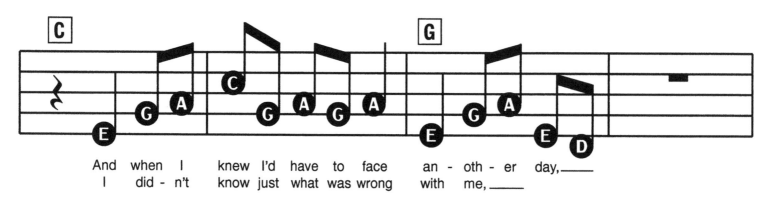

And when I knew I'd have to face an - oth - er day,_____
I did - n't know just what was wrong with me, _____

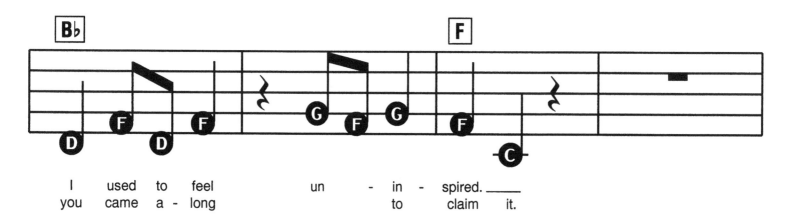

Lord, it made me feel so tired. _____
'til your kiss _____ helped me name it.

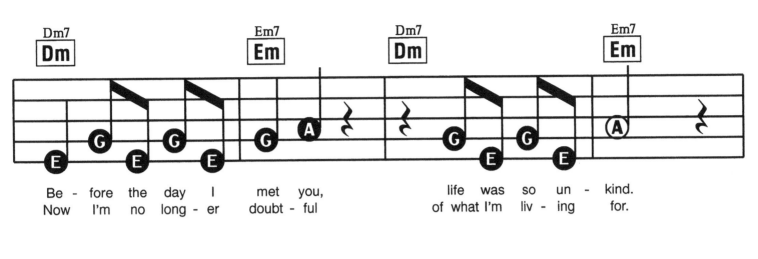

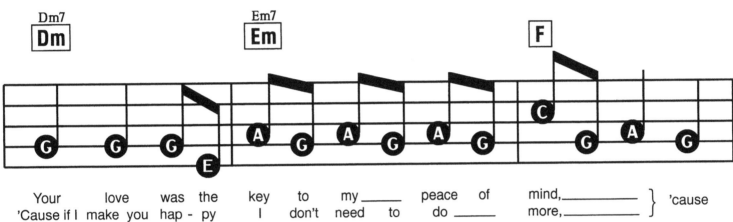

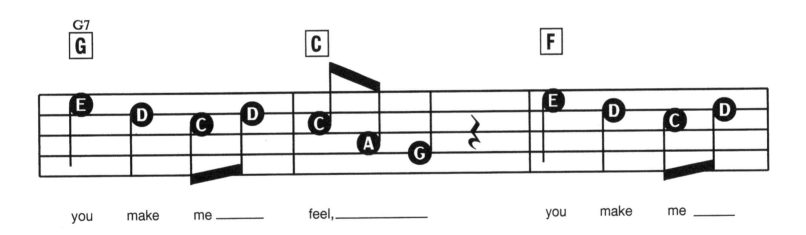

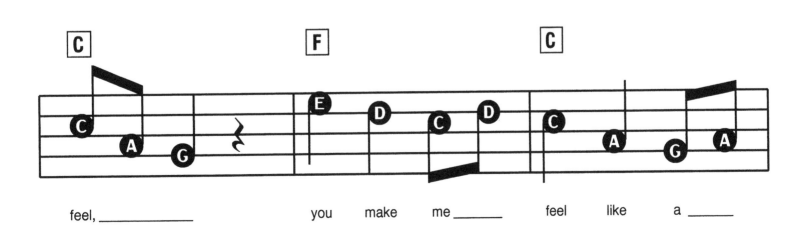

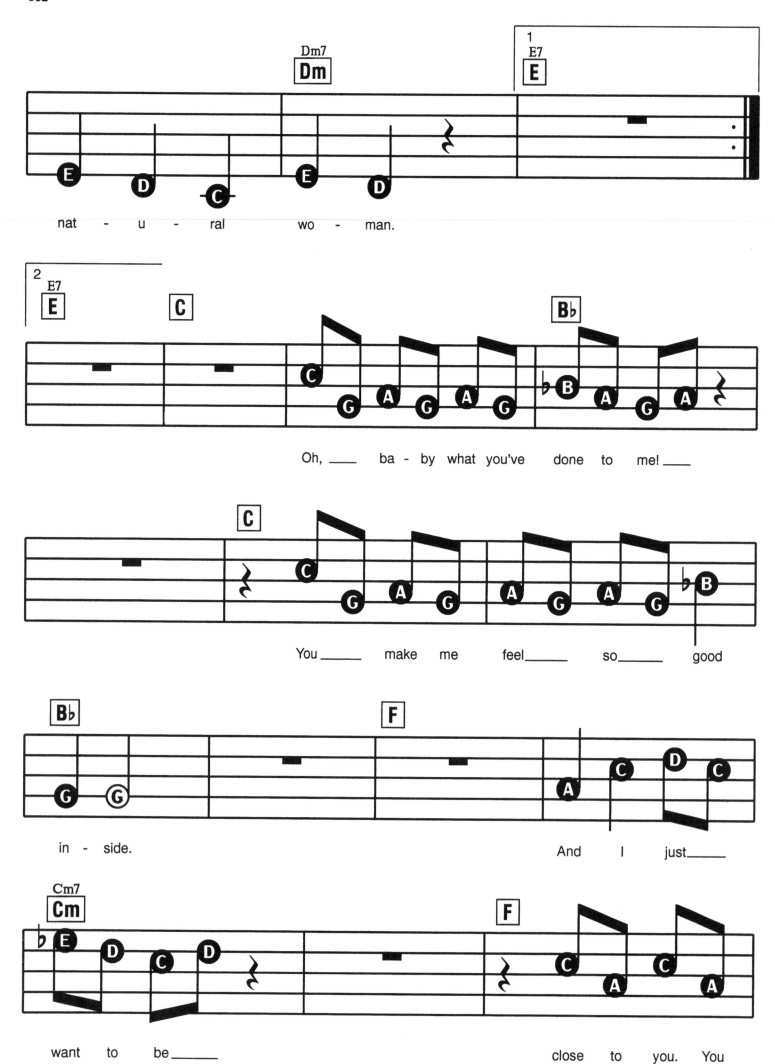

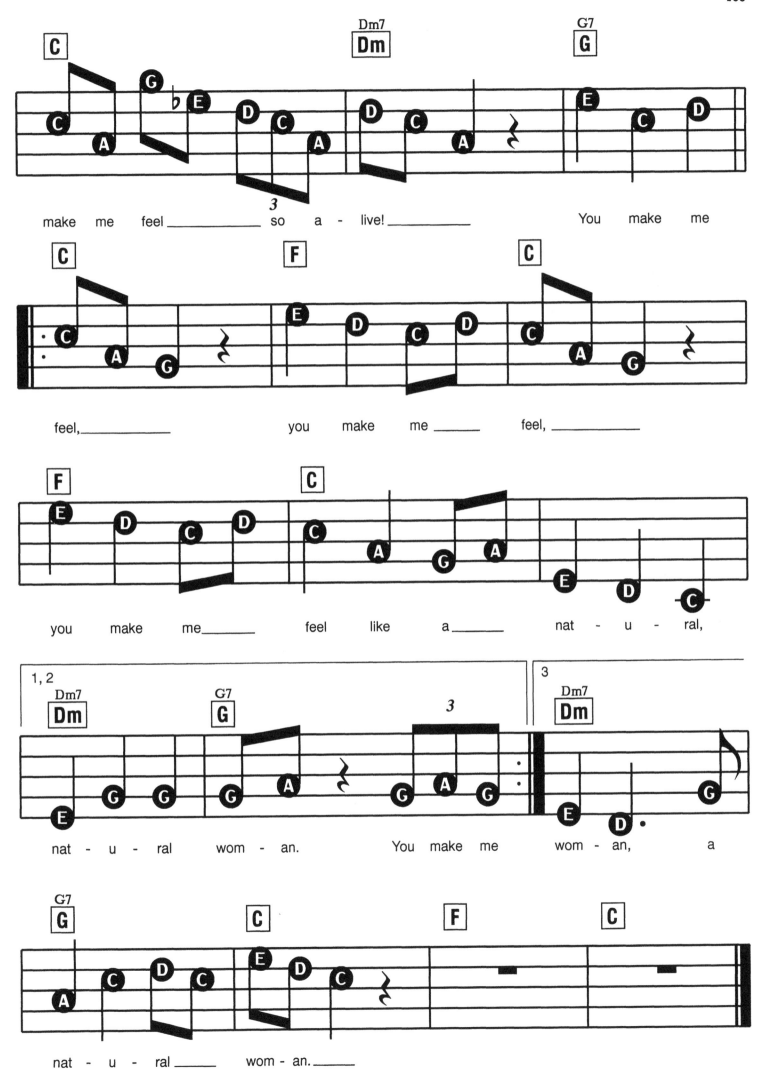

On Broadway

Registration 7
Rhythm: Rock

Words and Music by Barry Mann, Cynthia Weil,
Mike Stoller and Jerry Leiber

They say the ne - on lights are bright on
They say the wom - en treat you fine on
They say that I won't last too long on

Broad - way; _____
Broad - way; _____
Broad - way; _____

They say there's al - ways
But look - in' at them
I'll catch a Grey - hound

mag - ic in the air; _____
just gives me the blues; _____
bus for home, they say; _____

But when you're walk - in' down the street, And you ain't had e -
Cause how ya gon - na make some time, When all you got is
But they're dead wrong, I know they are, 'Cause I can play this

105

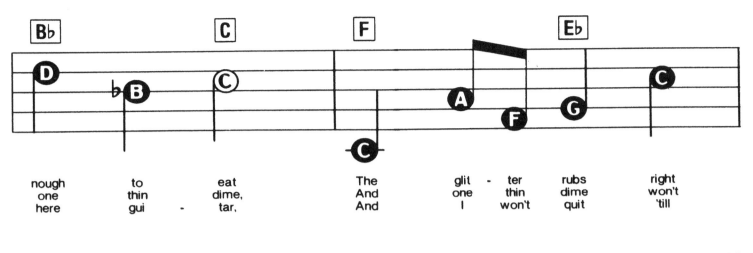

nough   to   eat
one   thin   dime,
here   gui - tar,   The   glit - ter   rubs   right
And   one   thin   dime   won't
And   I   won't   quit   'till

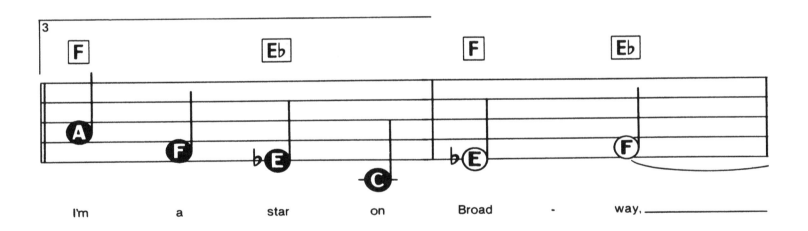

off   and   you're   no - where
e - ven   shine   your   shoes.

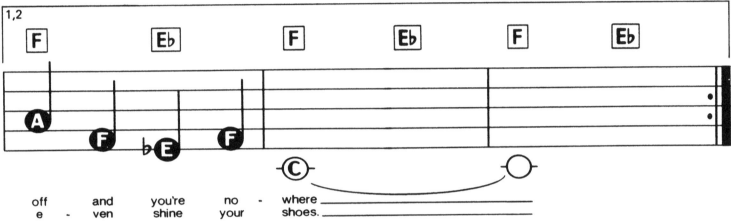

I'm   a   star   on   Broad - way,

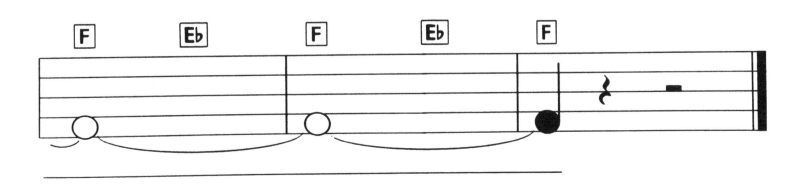

Only the Lonely
(Know the Way I Feel)

Registration 2
Rhythm: Rock or 8 Beat

Words and Music by Roy Orbison
and Joe Melson

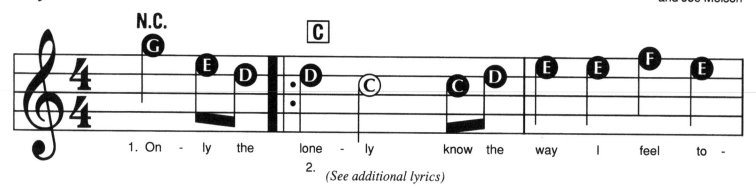

1. On - ly the lone - ly know the way I feel to -
2. (See additional lyrics)

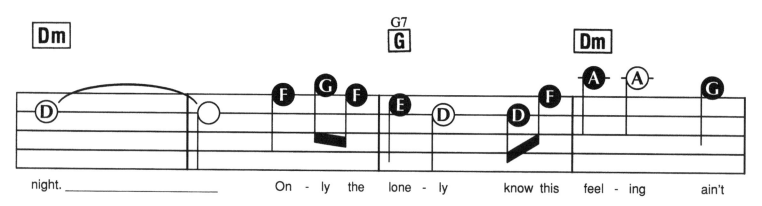

night. _____ On - ly the lone - ly know this feel - ing ain't

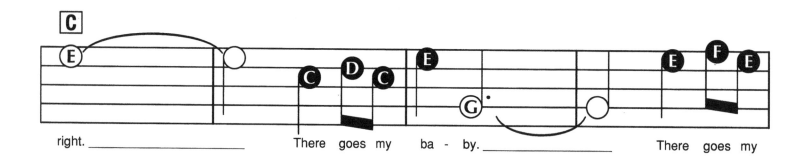

right. _____ There goes my ba - by. _____ There goes my

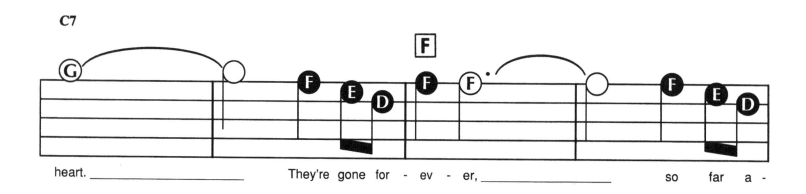

heart. _____ They're gone for - ev - er, _____ so far a -

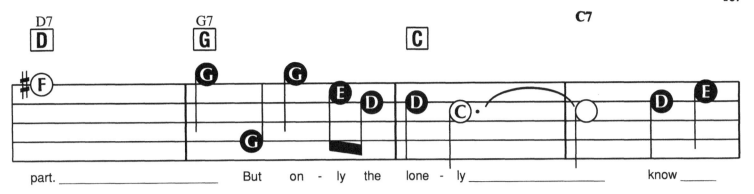

part. _____ But on - ly the lone - ly _____ know _____

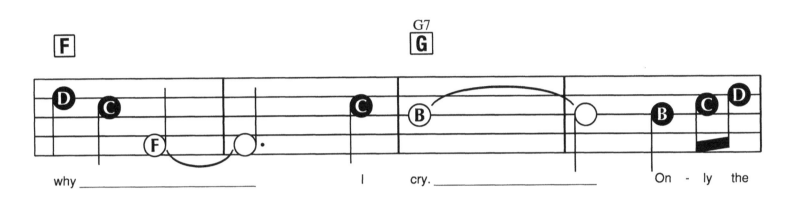

why _____ I cry. _____ On - ly the

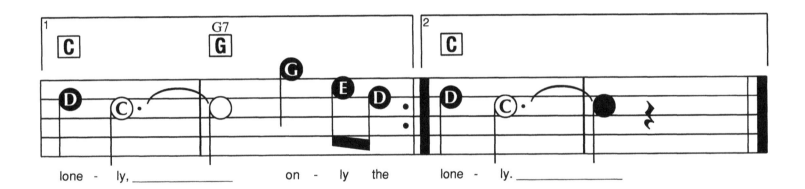

lone - ly, _____ on - ly the lone - ly. _____

Additional Lyrics

2. Only the lonely know the heartaches I've been through.
   Only the lonely know I cry and cry for you.
   Maybe tomorrow, a new romance,
   No more sorrow, but that's the chance
   You've got to take if you're lonely,
   Hearbreak, only the lonely.

Please Mr. Postman

Registration 1
Rhythm: Slow Rock or 12 Beat

Words and Music by Robert Bateman, Georgia Dobbins,
William Garrett, Freddie Gorman and Brian Holland

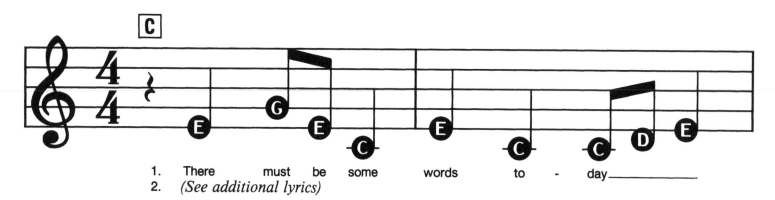

1. There must be some words to - day_____
2. *(See additional lyrics)*

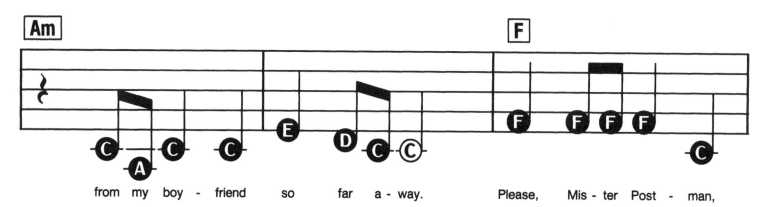

from my boy - friend so far a - way.   Please,   Mis - ter Post - man,

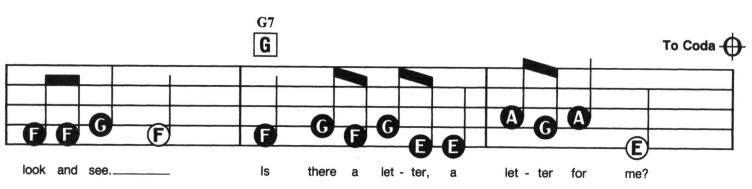

look and see._____   Is   there a let - ter,   a   let - ter for   me?

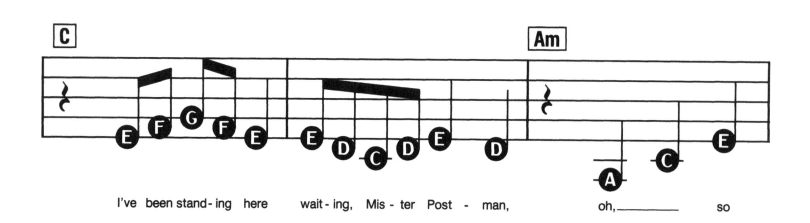

I've been stand - ing here   wait - ing, Mis - ter Post - man,   oh,_____   so

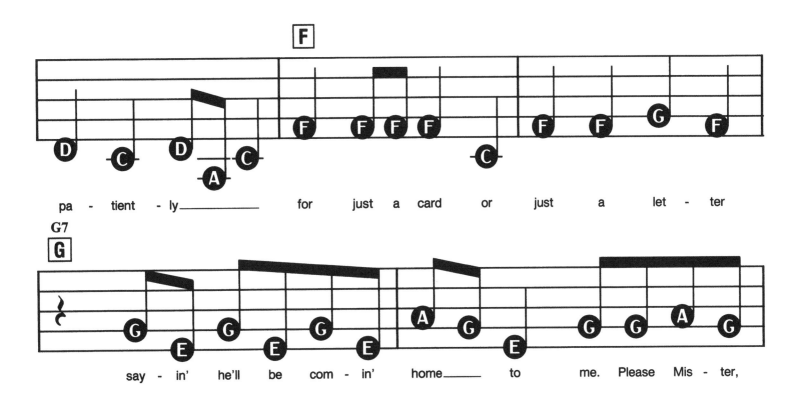

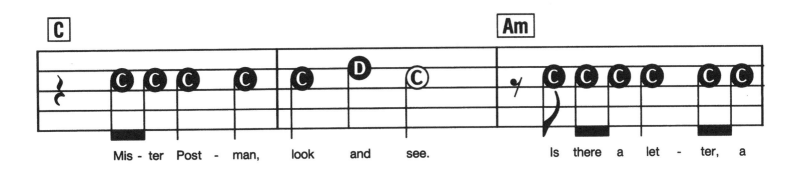

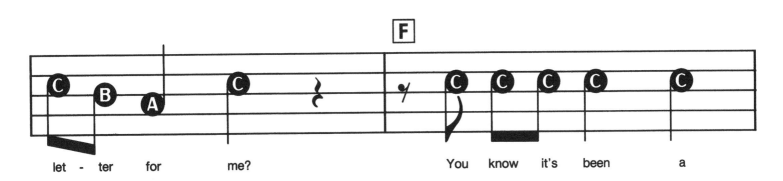

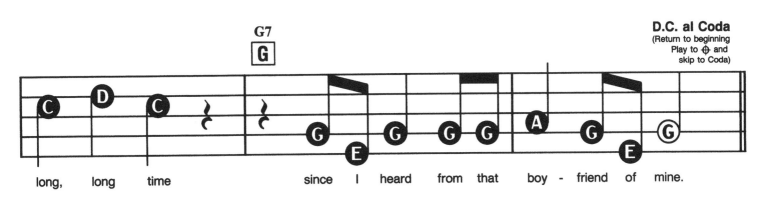

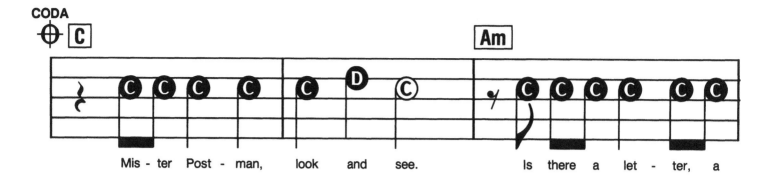

Mis - ter Post - man, look and see. Is there a let - ter, a

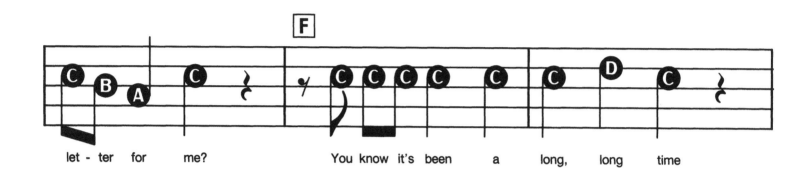

let - ter for me? You know it's been a long, long time

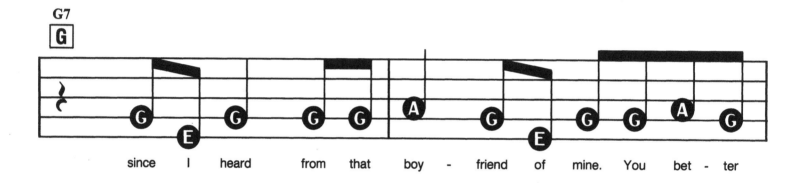

since I heard from that boy - friend of mine. You bet - ter

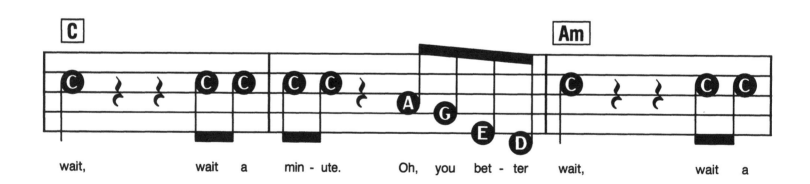

wait, wait a min - ute. Oh, you bet - ter wait, wait a

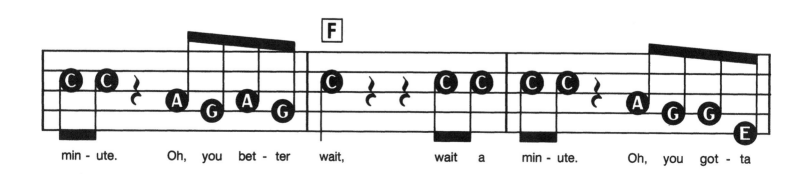

min - ute. Oh, you bet - ter wait, wait a min - ute. Oh, you got - ta

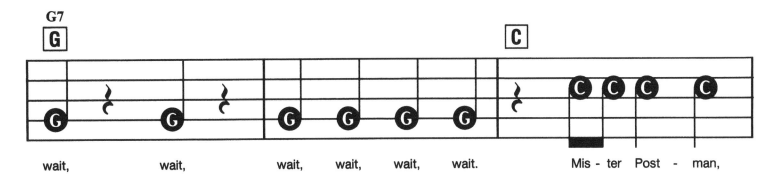

wait, wait, wait, wait, wait, wait. Mis - ter Post - man,

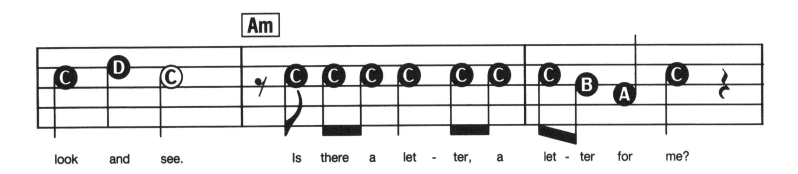

look and see. Is there a let - ter, a let - ter for me?

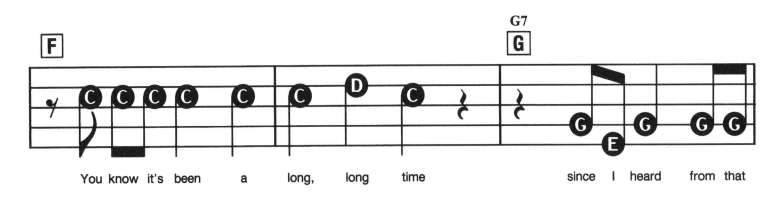

You know it's been a long, long time since I heard from that

Repeat and Fade

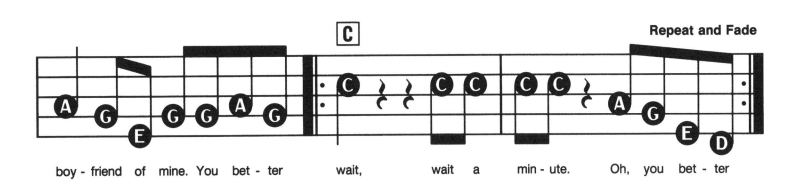

boy - friend of mine. You bet - ter wait, wait a min - ute. Oh, you bet - ter

ADDITIONAL LYRICS

2. So many days have passed me by.
   You saw the tears in my eyes.
   You wouldn't stop to make me feel better
   By leavin' me a card or a letter.

Please Please Me

Registration 8
Rhythm: Rock

Words and Music by John Lennon
and Paul McCartney

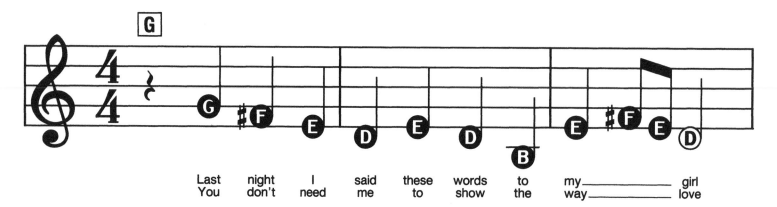

Last night I said these words to my_____ girl
You don't need me to show the way_____ love

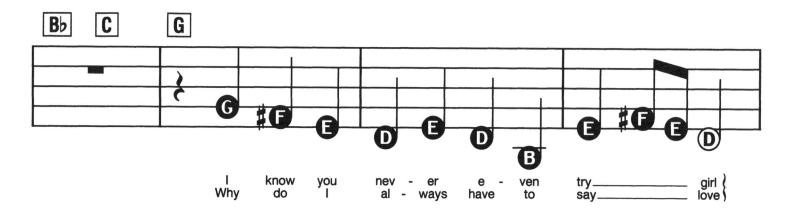

I know you nev - er e - ven try_____ girl
Why do I al - ways have to say_____ love

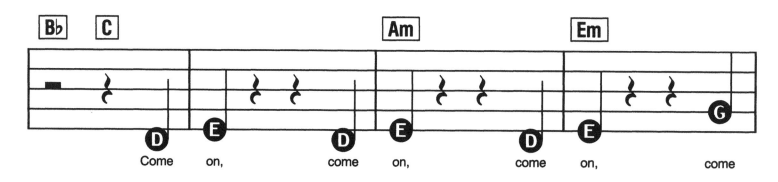

Come on, come on, come on, come

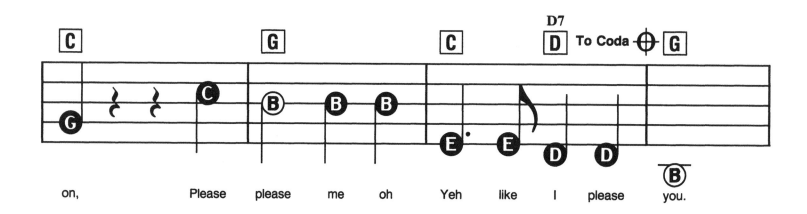

on, Please please me oh Yeh like I please you.

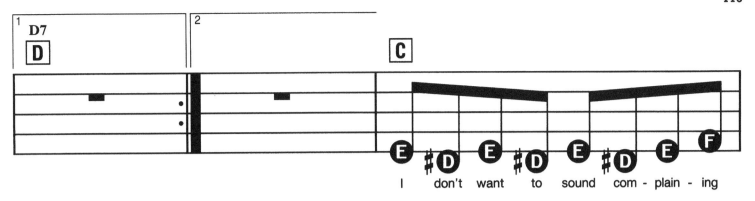

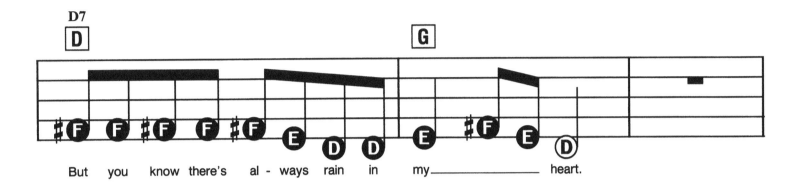

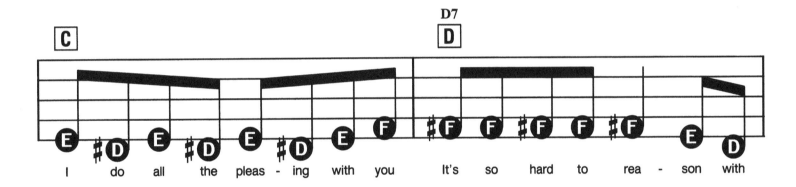

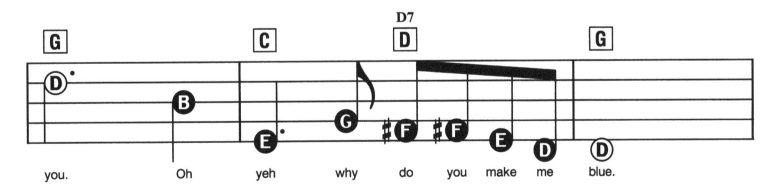

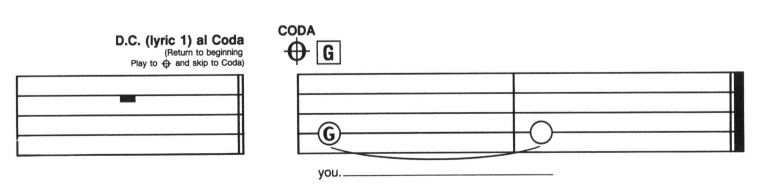

Reason to Believe

Registration 7
Rhythm: Rock or 8 Beat

Words and Music by
Tim Hardin

If I lis - tened long e - nough to you I'd find a
If I gave you time to change my mind I'd find a

way to be - lieve that it's all _____ true,
way to leave the the past be - hind,

Know - ing that you lied straight - faced while I cried, still I'd
Know - ing that you lied straight - faced while I cried, still I'd

look to find a rea - son to be - lieve.
look to find a rea - son to be - lieve.

Some - one like

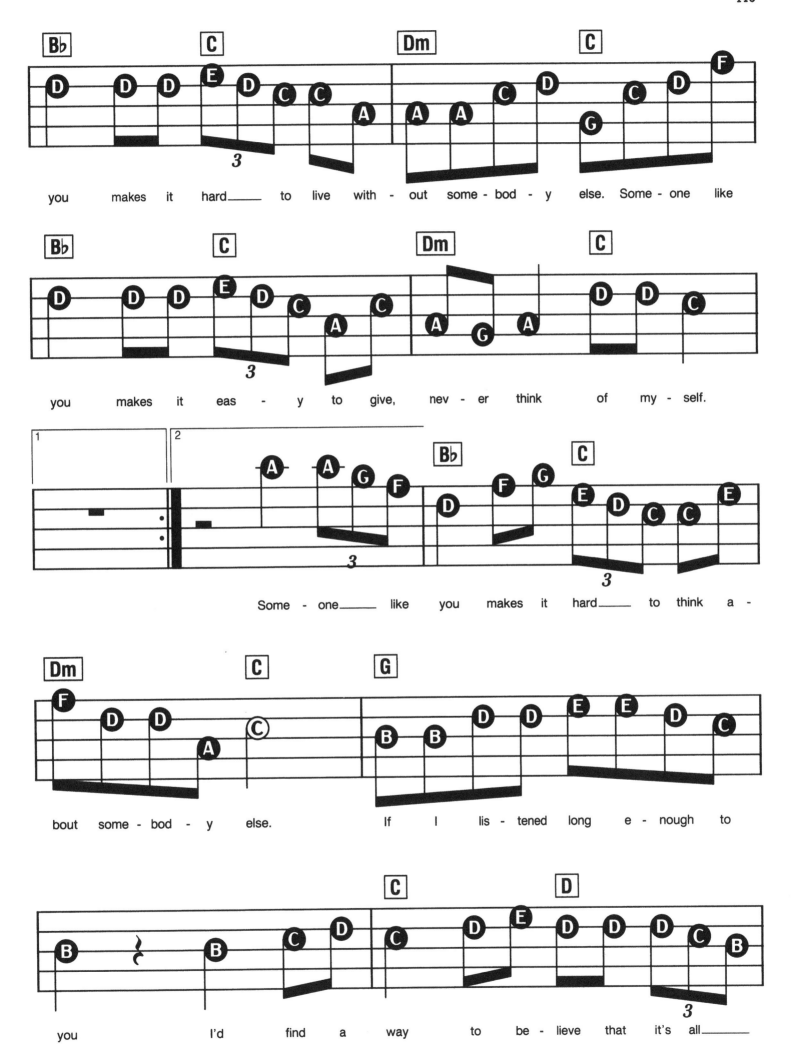

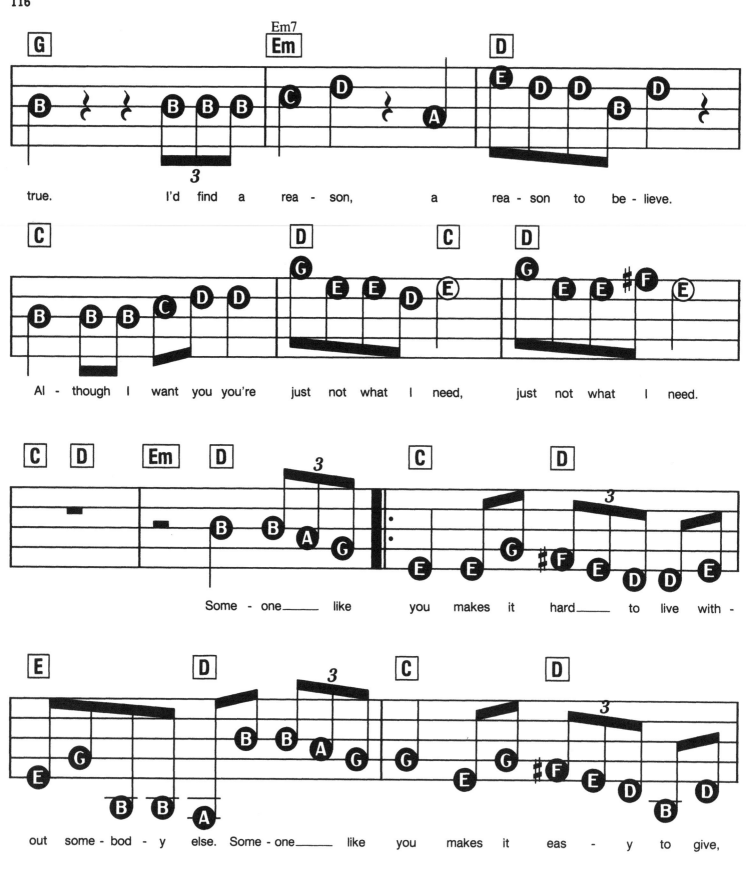

true.   I'd find a rea - son,   a rea - son to be - lieve.

Al - though I want you you're   just not what I need,   just not what I need.

Some - one____ like   you makes it hard____ to live with -

out some - bod - y else. Some - one____ like   you makes it eas - y to give,

Repeat and Fade

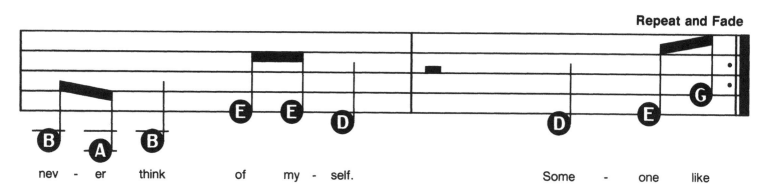

nev - er think   of my - self.   Some - one like

(You're My)
Soul and Inspiration

Registration 3
Rhythm: Rock or 8 Beat

Words and Music by Barry Mann
and Cynthia Weil

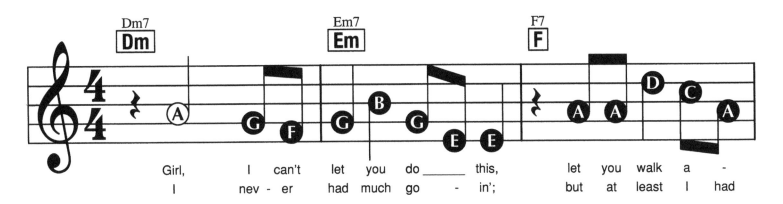

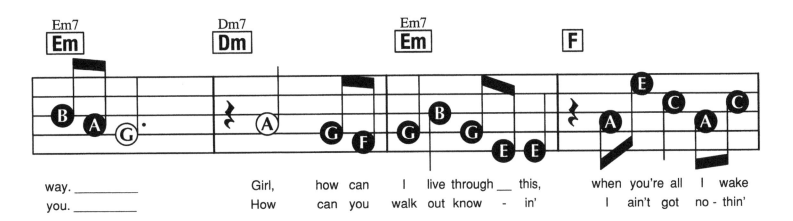

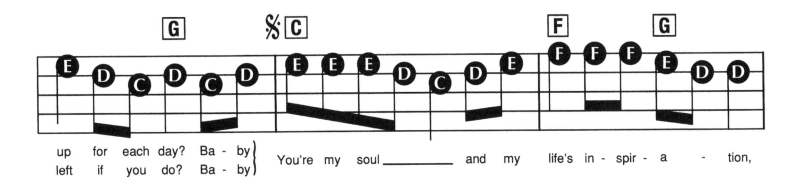

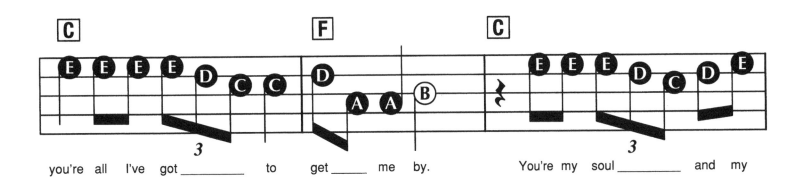

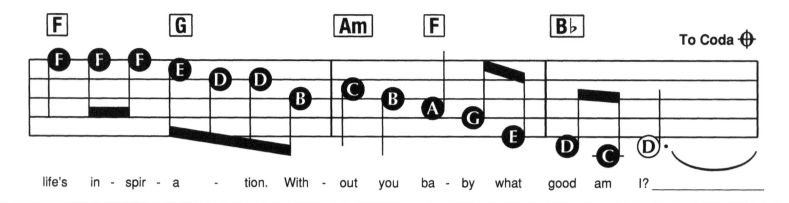

To Coda ⊕

life's in - spir - a - tion. With - out you ba - by what good am I? _____

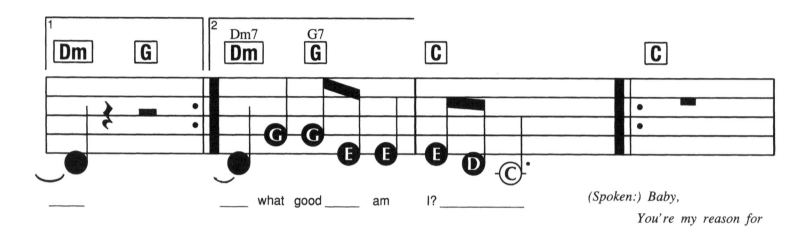

_____ _____ what good _____ am I? _____

(Spoken:) Baby,
You're my reason for

I can't make it without you and I'm, I'm tellin' you honey that, Ba - by _____
laughin' and for cryin', for livin' and dyin'.

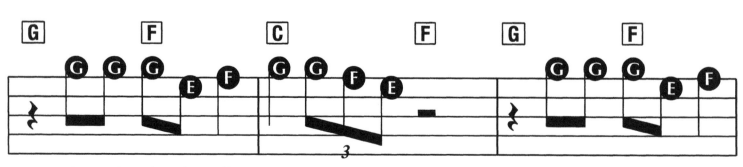

I can't make it with - out you. _____ Please I'm beg - gin' you

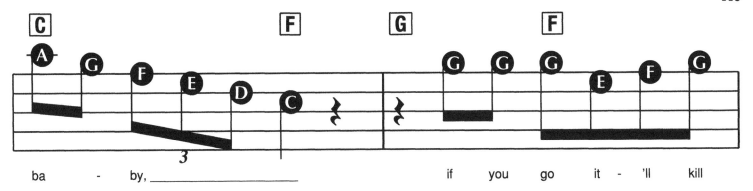

ba - by, _____ if you go it - 'll kill

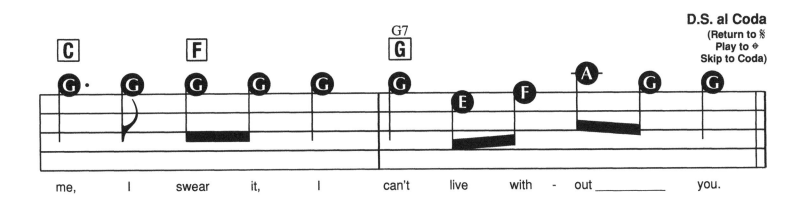

D.S. al Coda
(Return to %
Play to ⊕
Skip to Coda)

me, I swear it, I can't live with - out _____ you.

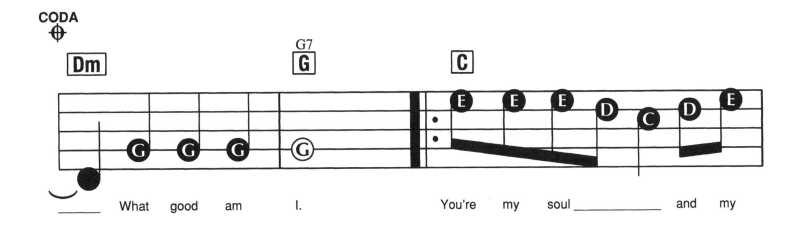

CODA
⊕

_____ What good am I. You're my soul _____ and my

Repeat and Fade

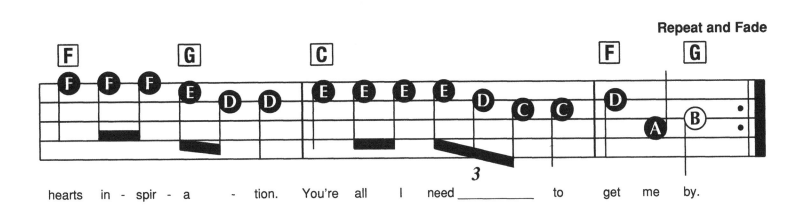

hearts in - spir - a - tion. You're all I need _____ to get me by.

Return to Sender

Registration 4
Rhythm: Rock

Words and Music by Otis Blackwell
and Winfield Scott

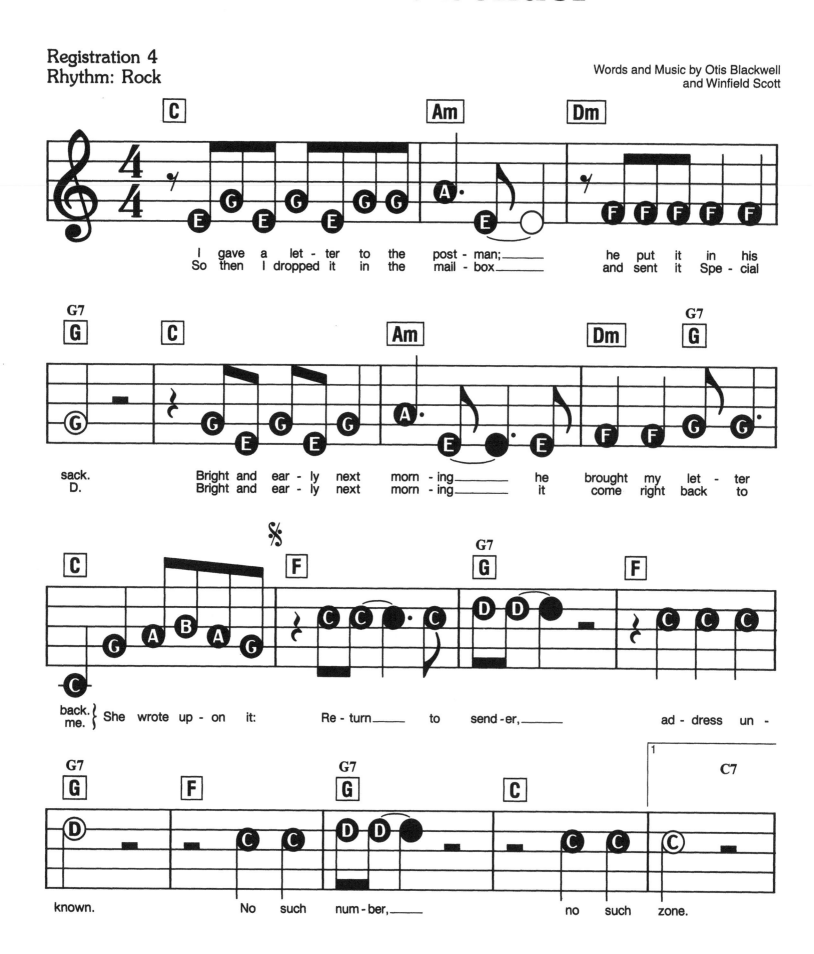

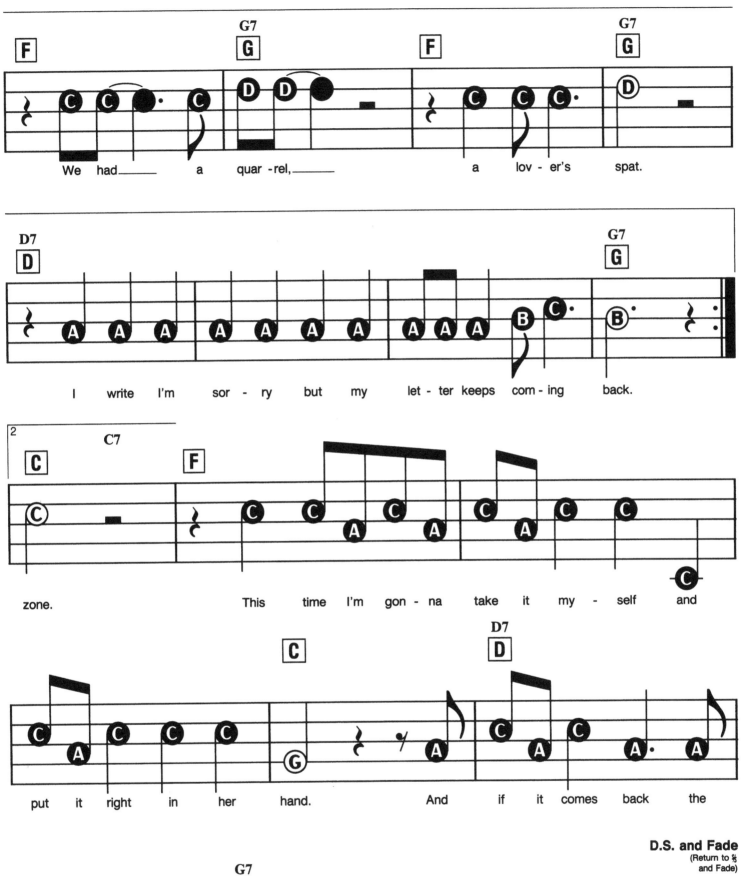

We had_____ a quar -rel,_____ a lov - er's spat.

I write I'm sor - ry but my let - ter keeps com - ing back.

zone. This time I'm gon - na take it my - self and

put it right in her hand. And if it comes back the

D.S. and Fade
(Return to %
and Fade)

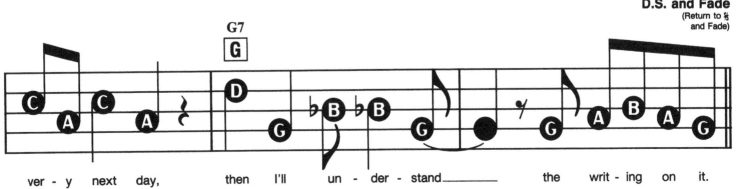

ver - y next day, then I'll un - der - stand_____ the writ - ing on it.

Spinning Wheel

Registration 7
Rhythm: Rock

Words and Music by
David Clayton Thomas

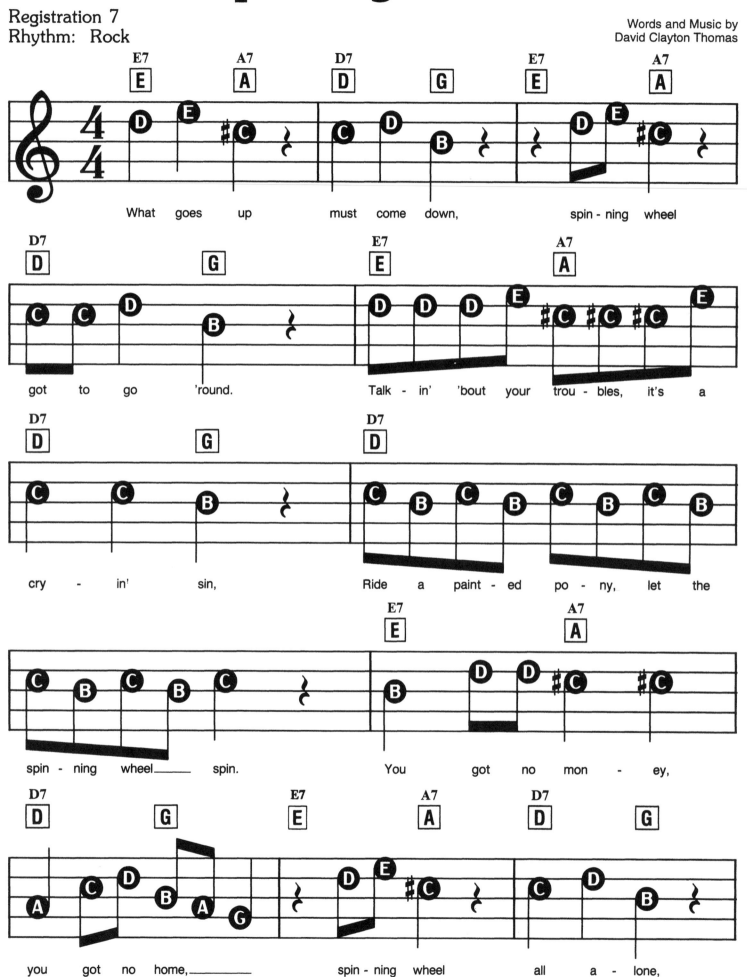

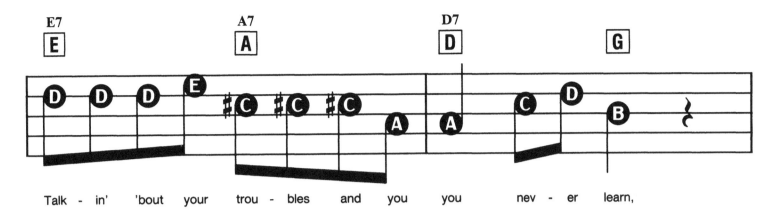

Talk - in' 'bout your trou - bles and you you nev - er learn,

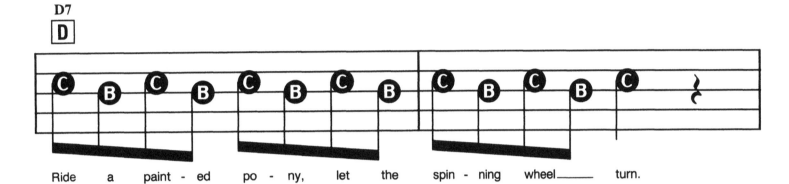

Ride a paint - ed po - ny, let the spin - ning wheel___ turn.

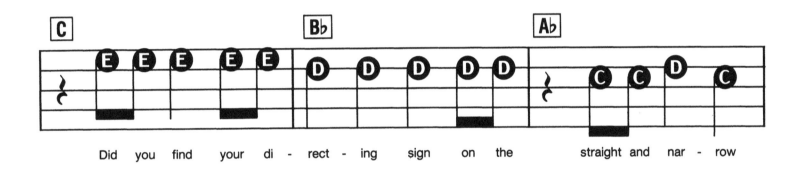

Did you find your di - rect - ing sign on the straight and nar - row

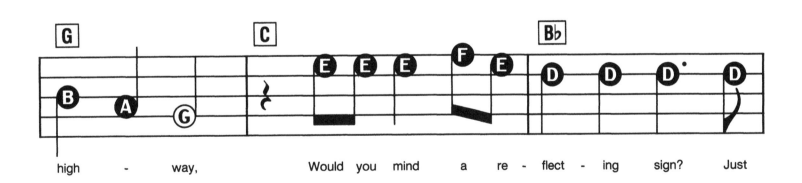

high - way, Would you mind a re - flect - ing sign? Just

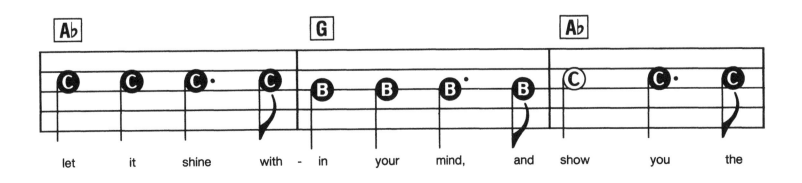

let it shine with - in your mind, and show you the

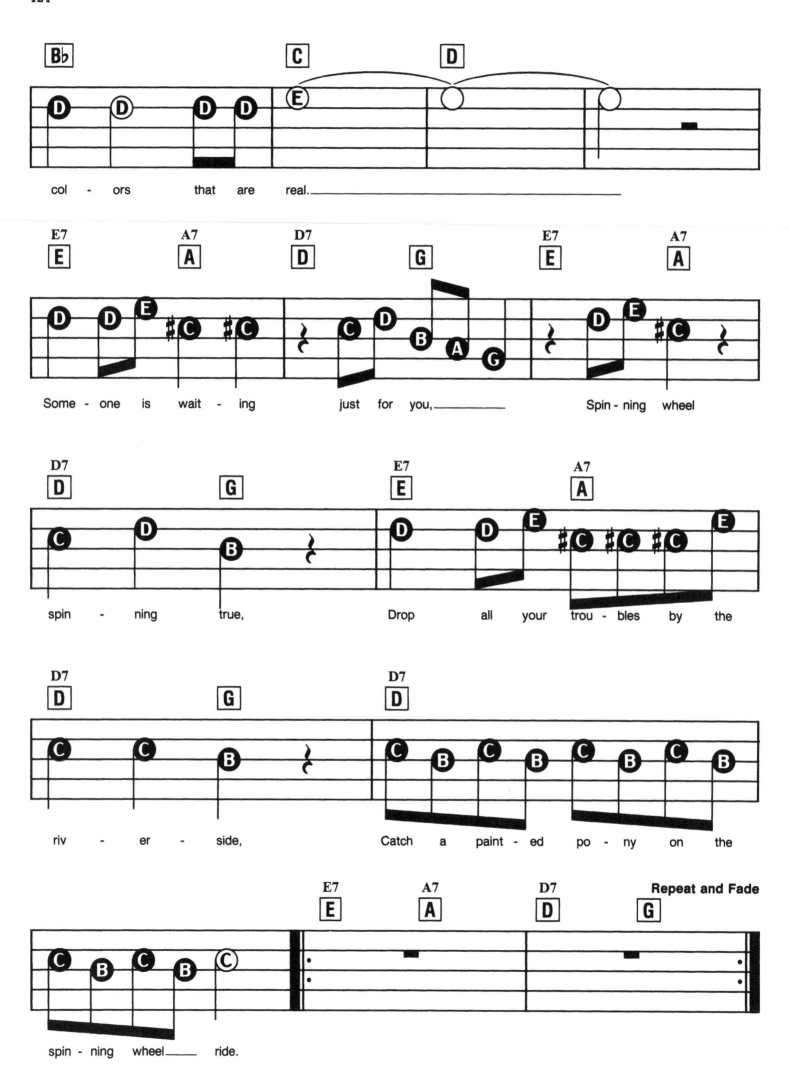

Stop! In the Name of Love

Registration 8
Rhythm: Rock or Pops

Words and Music by Lamont Dozier,
Brian Holland and Edward Holland

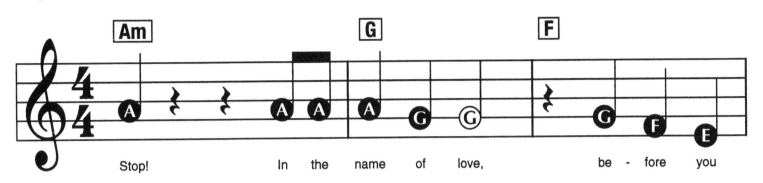

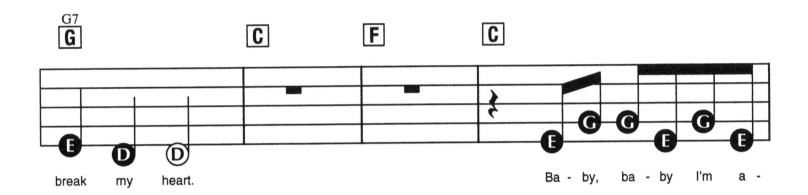

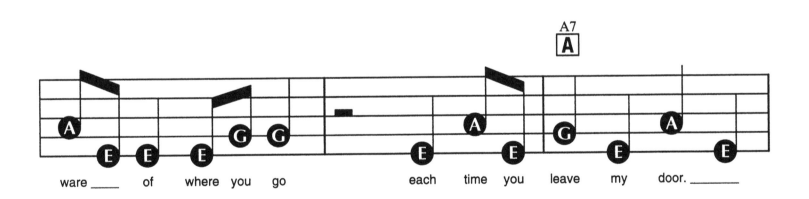

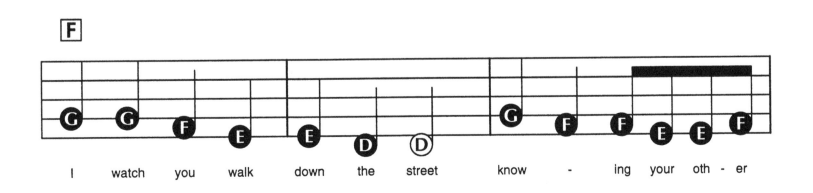

126

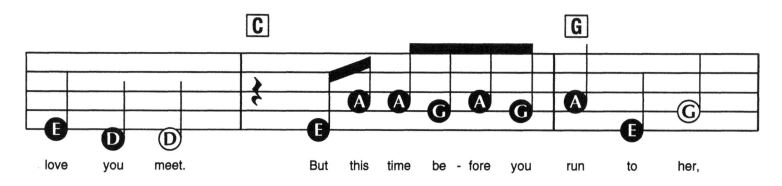

love you meet. But this time be - fore you run to her,

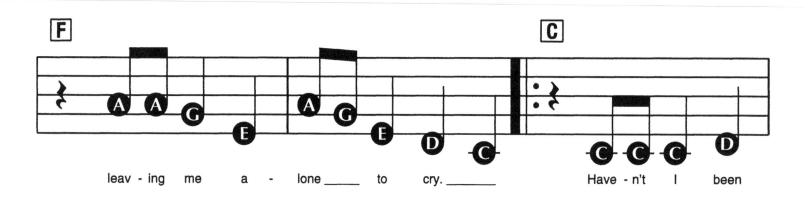

leav - ing me a - lone ___ to cry. ___ Have - n't I been

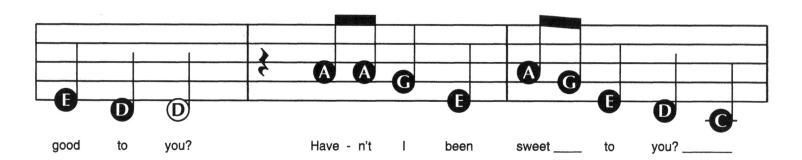

good to you? Have - n't I been sweet ___ to you? ___

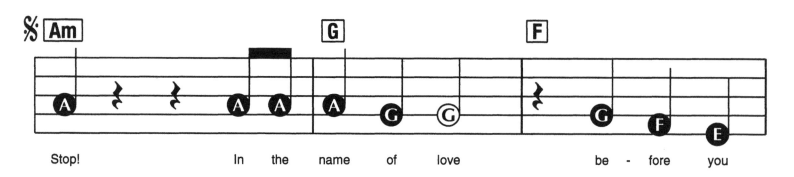

Stop! In the name of love be - fore you

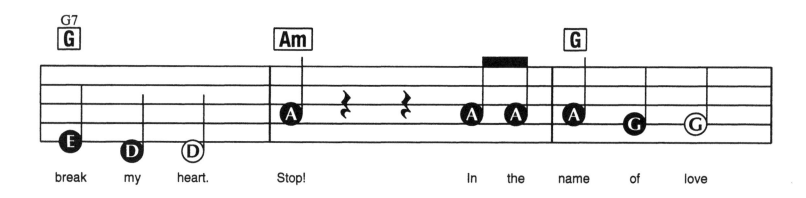

break my heart. Stop! In the name of love

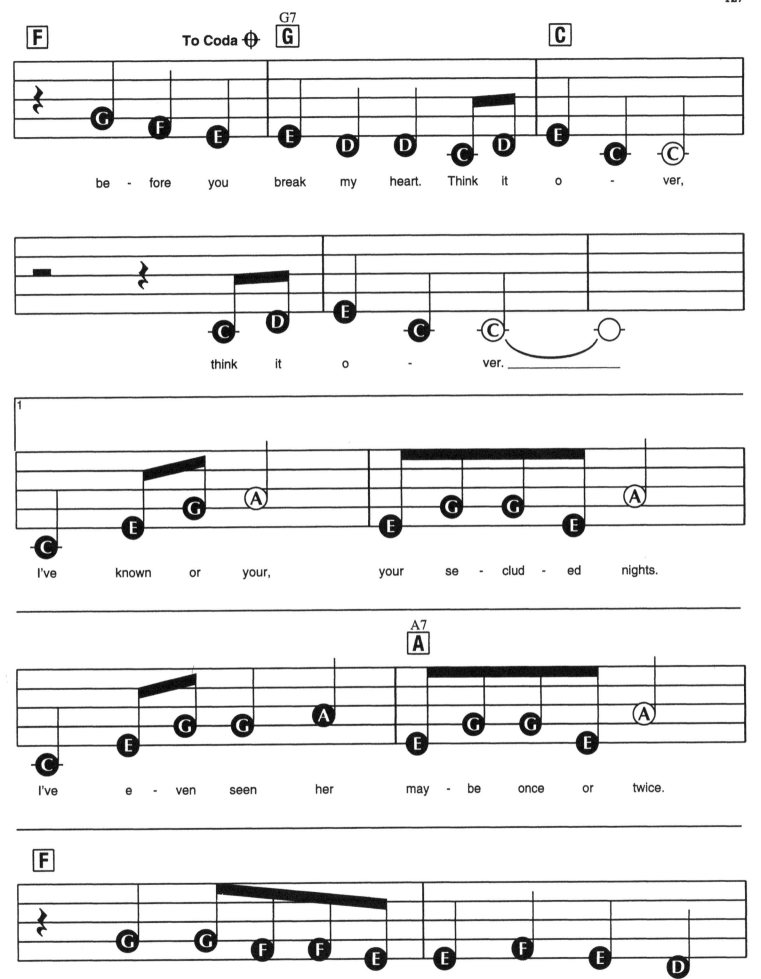

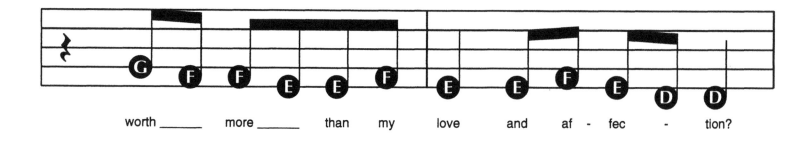

worth _____ more _____ than my love and af - fec - tion?

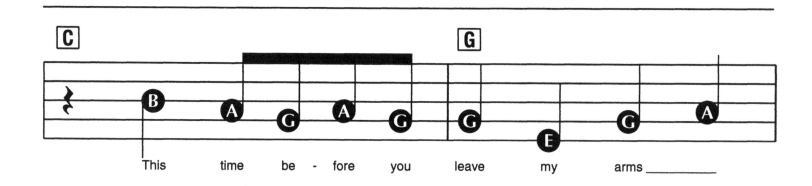

This time be - fore you leave my arms _____

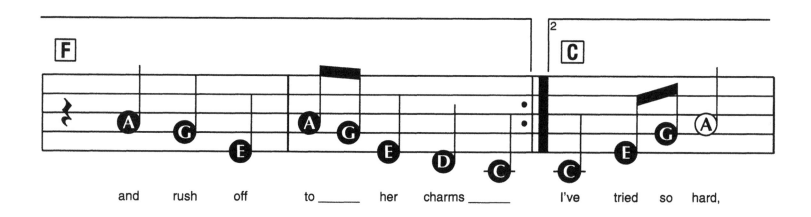

and rush off to _____ her charms _____ I've tried so hard,

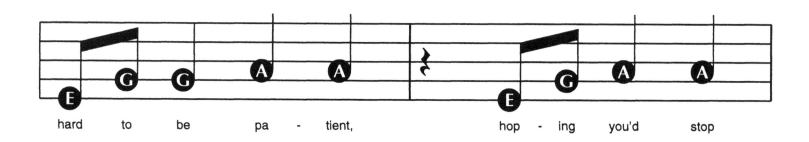

hard to be pa - tient, hop - ing you'd stop

129

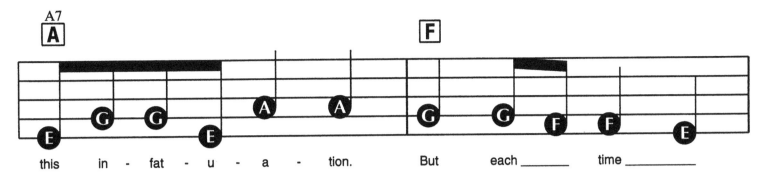

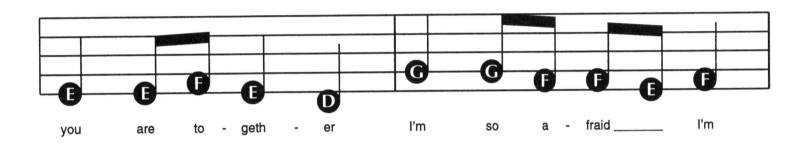

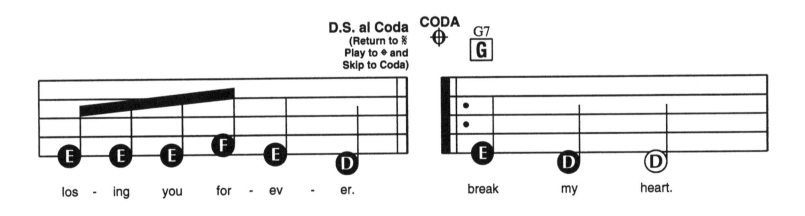

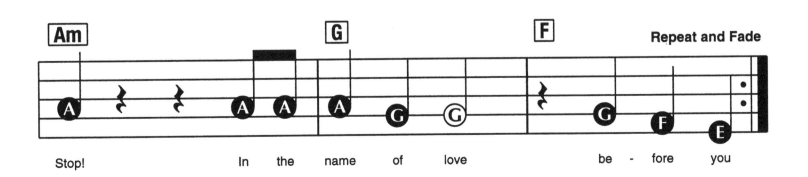

Sugar, Sugar

Registration 1
Rhythm: Rock

Words and Music by Andy Kim
and Jeff Barry

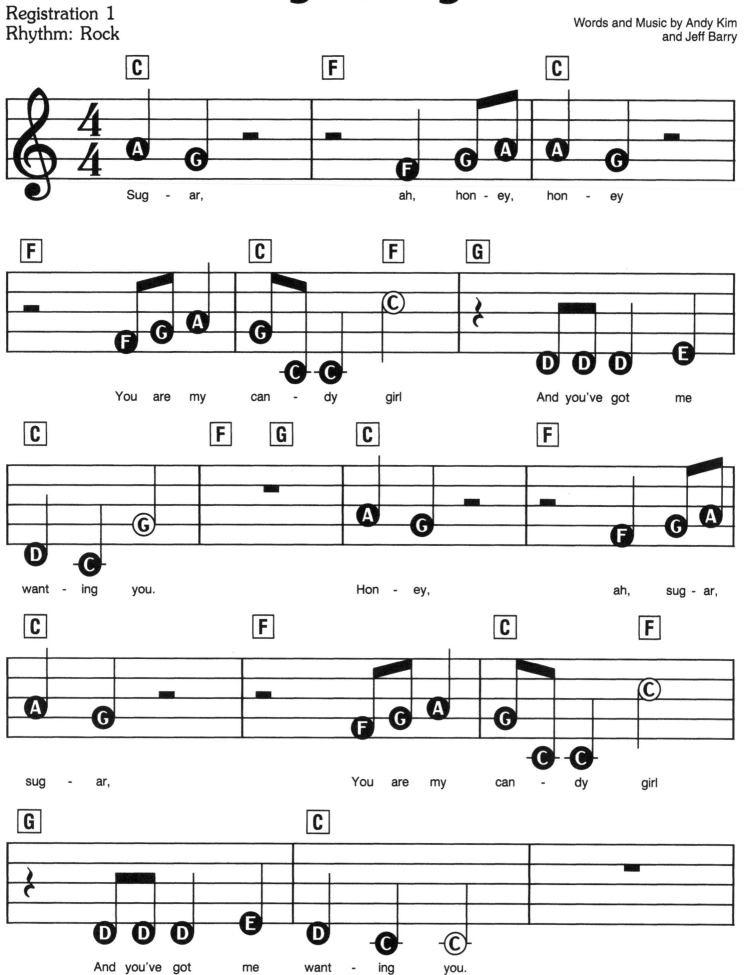

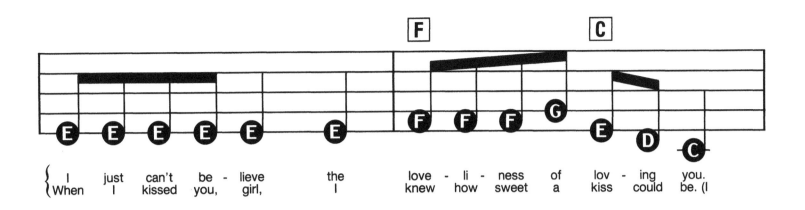

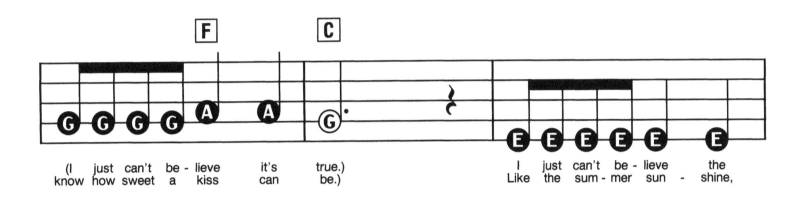

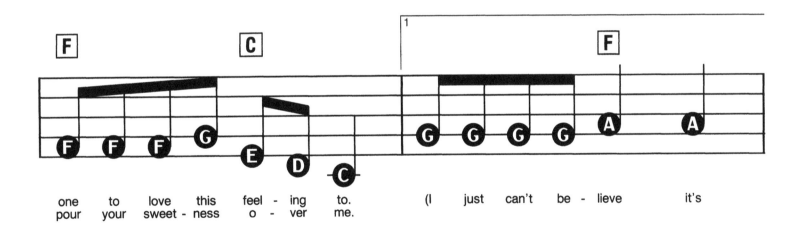

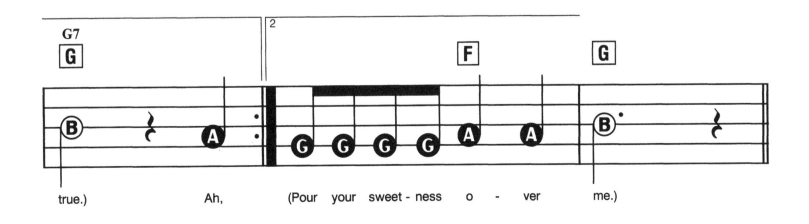

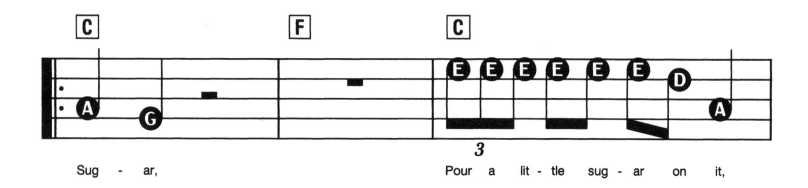

Sug - ar,   Pour a lit - tle sug - ar on it,

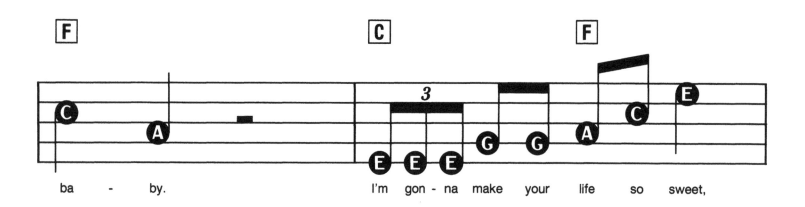

ba - by.   I'm gon - na make your life so sweet,

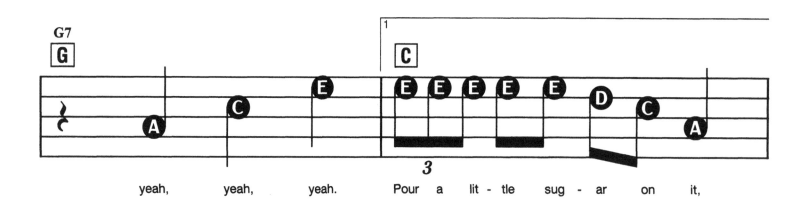

yeah, yeah, yeah.   Pour a lit - tle sug - ar on it,

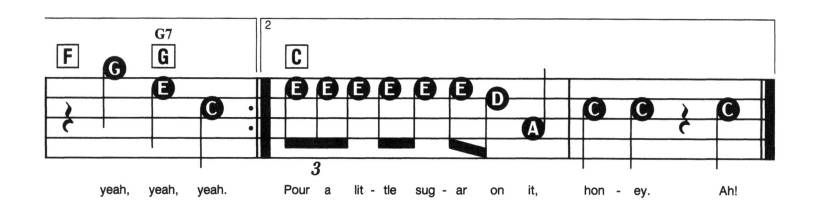

yeah, yeah, yeah.   Pour a lit - tle sug - ar on it, hon - ey.   Ah!

Suspicious Minds

Registration 7
Rhythm: Rock

Words and Music by
Mark James

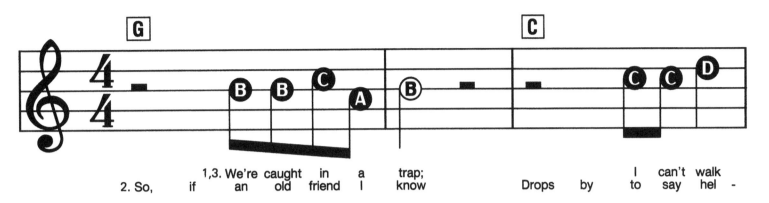

1,3. We're caught in a trap;
2. So, if an old friend I know

I can't walk

Drops by to say hel -

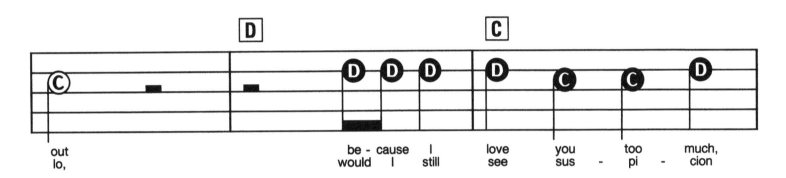

out
lo,

be - cause I
would I still

love you too much,
see sus - pi - cion

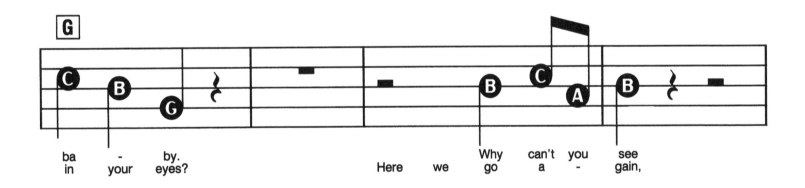

ba - by.
in your eyes?

Here we

Why can't you see
go a - gain,

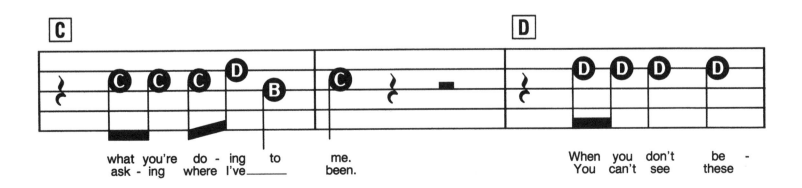

what you're do - ing to me.
ask - ing where I've been.

When you don't be -
You can't see these

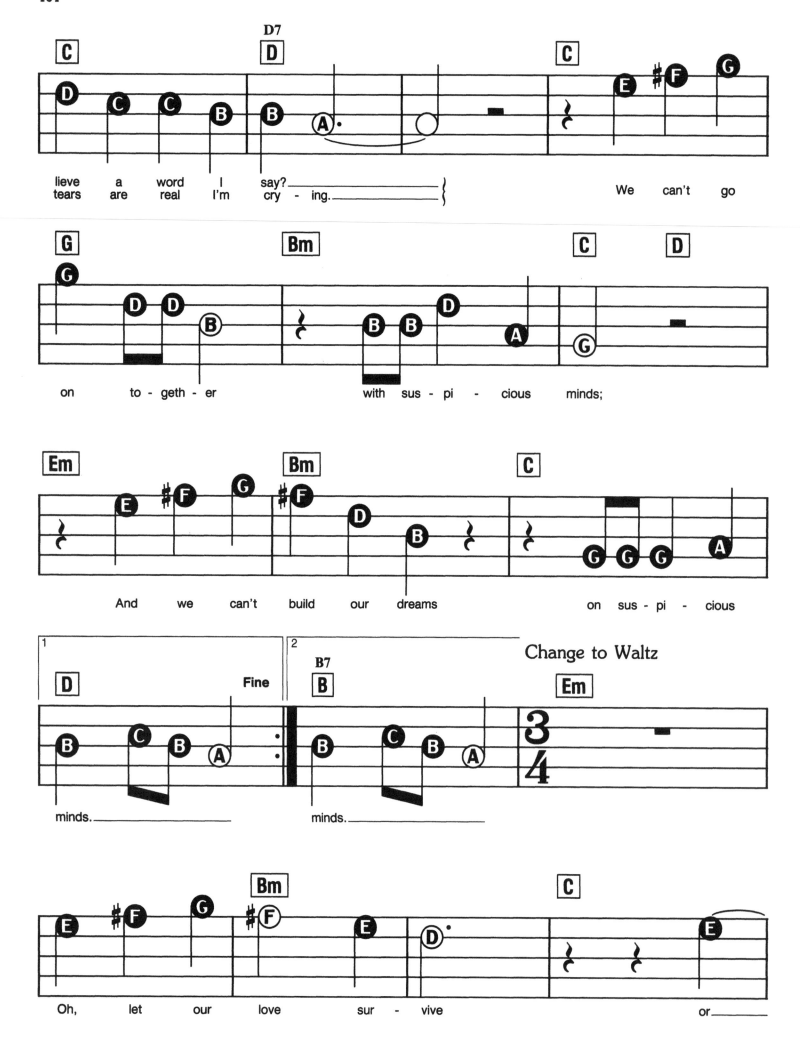

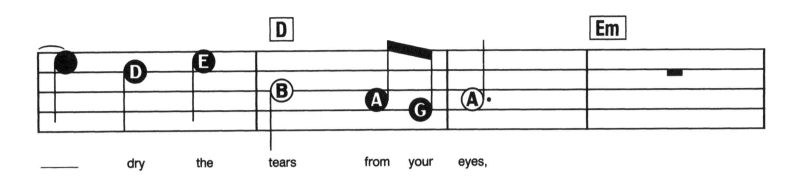

_____ dry the tears from your eyes,

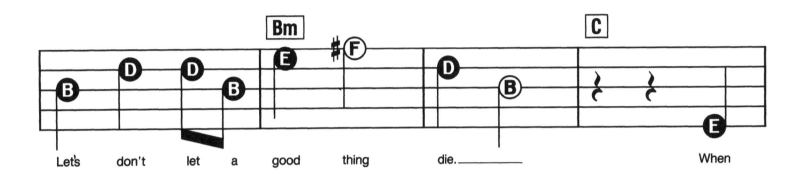

Let's don't let a good thing die. _____ When

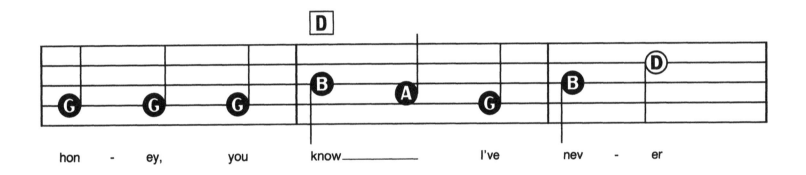

hon - ey, you know _____ I've nev - er

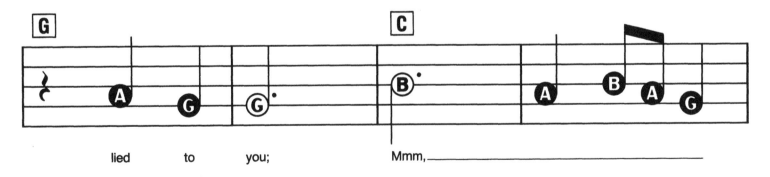

lied to you; Mmm, _____

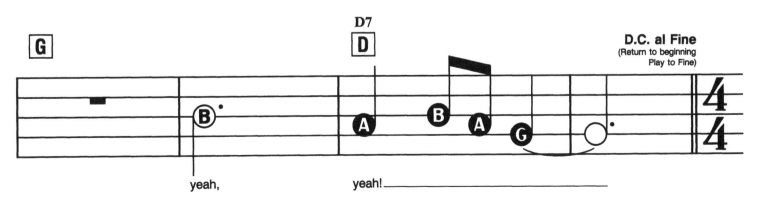

yeah, yeah! _____

True Grit

Registration 5
Rhythm: Pops, 8 Beat, or Rock

Words by Don Black
Music by Elmer Bernstein

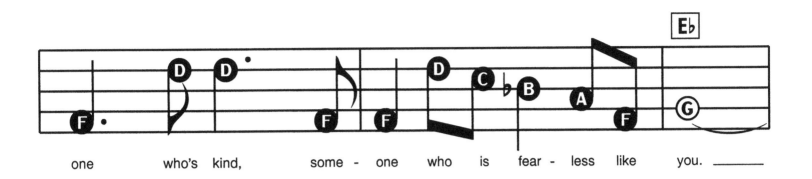

one   who's kind,   some - one   who   is   fear - less   like   you. _____

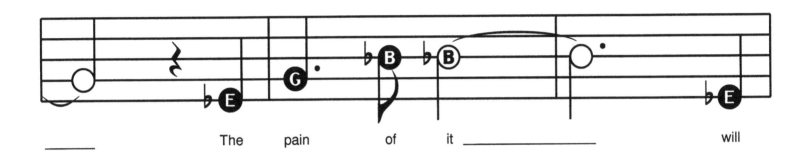

____   The   pain   of   it _____   will

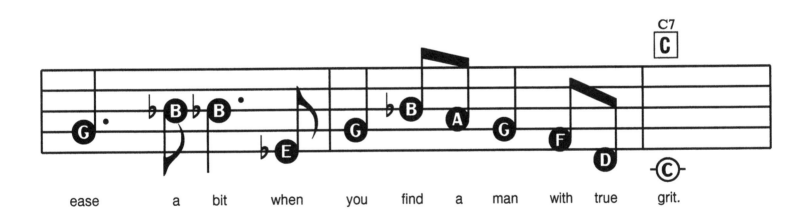

ease   a   bit   when   you   find   a   man   with   true   grit.

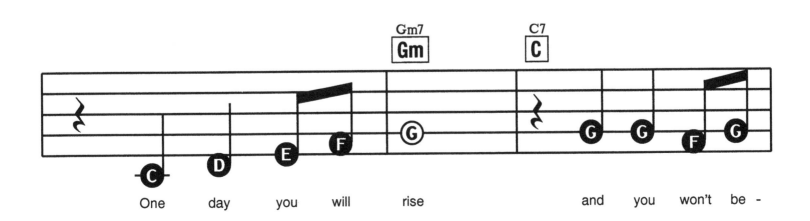

One   day   you   will   rise   and   you   won't   be -

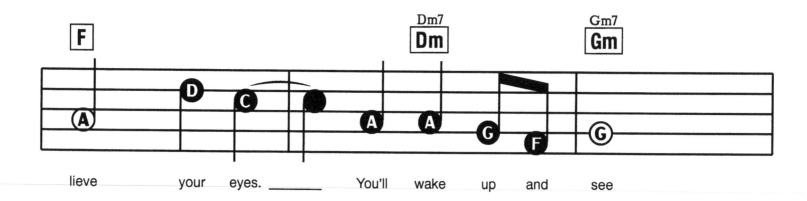

lieve your eyes. _____ You'll wake up and see

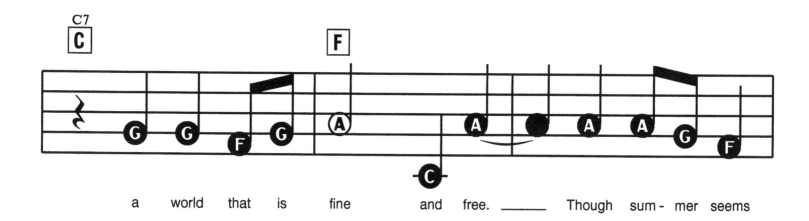

a world that is fine and free. _____ Though sum - mer seems

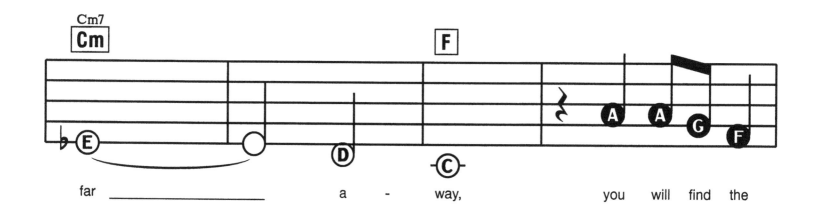

far _____ a - way, you will find the

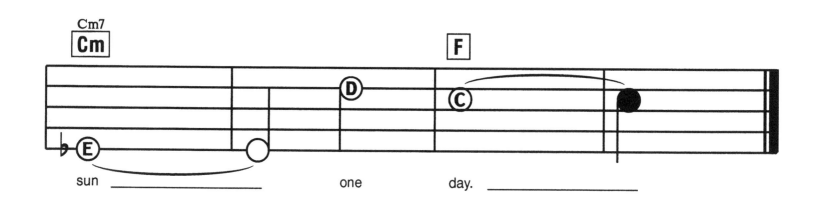

sun _____ one day. _____

Twist and Shout

Registration 4
Rhythm: Rock

Words and Music by Bert Russell
and Phil Medley

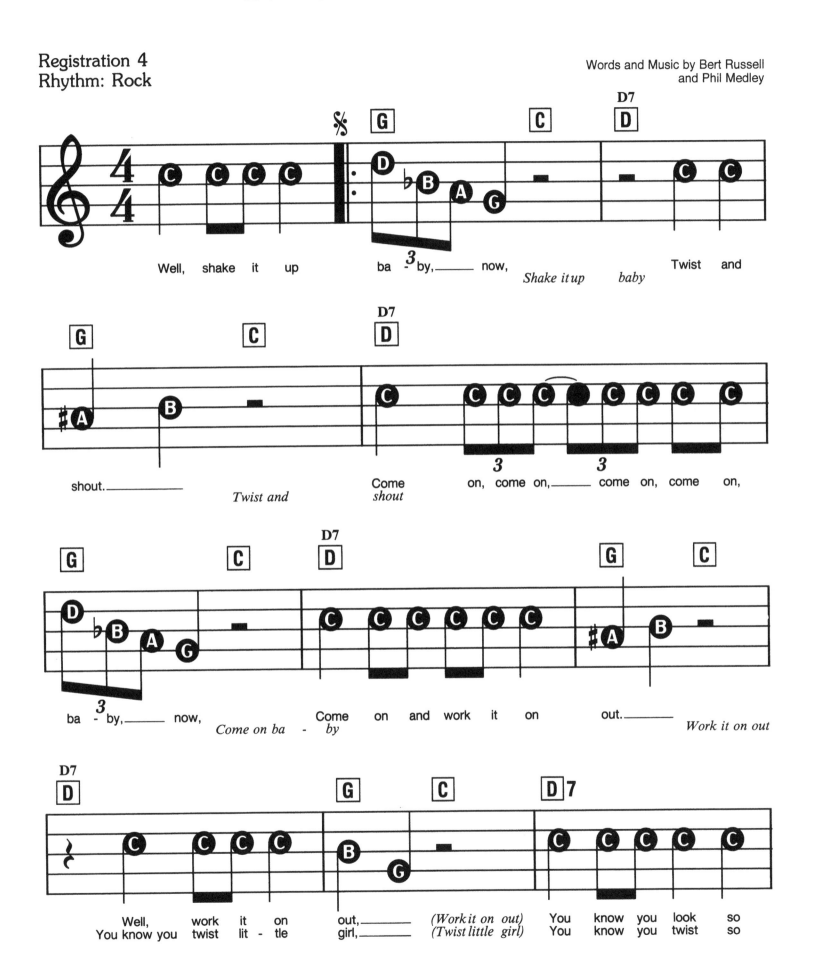

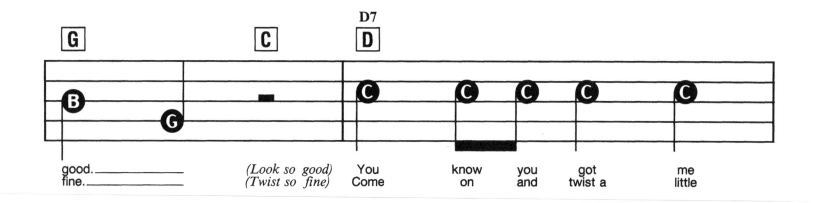

good. _____
fine. _____
(Look so good)
(Twist so fine)
You
Come
know
on
you
and
got
twist a
me
little

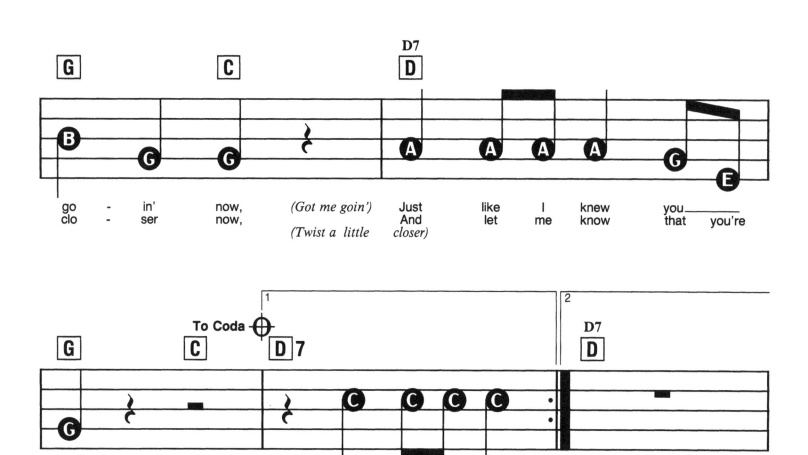

go - in' now,
clo - ser now,
(Got me goin')
(Twist a little
Just
And
closer)
like
let
I
me
knew
know
you _____
that
you're

To Coda

1.

would.
mine.
(Like I
(Let me
knew you
know you're
would)
Well,
shake
it
up

2.

mine.
oo)

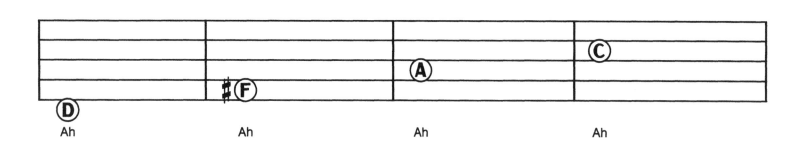

Ah
Ah
Ah
Ah

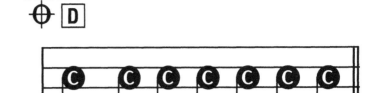

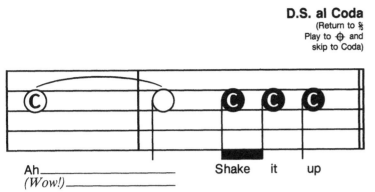

D.S. al Coda
(Return to ℅
Play to ⊕ and
skip to Coda)

Ah_____
*(Wow!)*_____

Shake it up

CODA D7

Well, shake it, shake it, shake it,

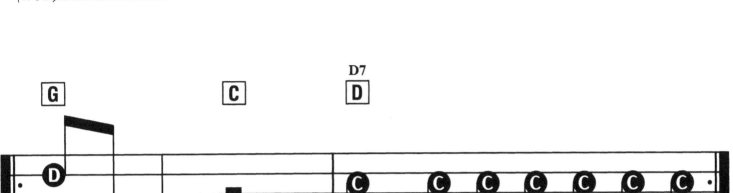

G **C** **D7** **D**

ba - by now, *shake it up*

Well, shake it, shake it, shake it,
baby

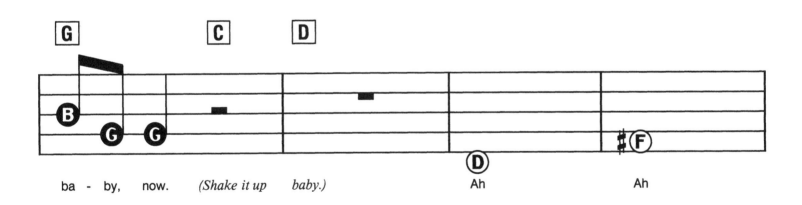

G **C** **D**

ba - by, now. *(Shake it up baby.)* Ah Ah

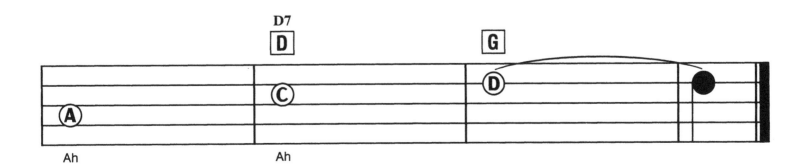

D7 **D** **G**

Ah Ah

Viva Las Vegas

Registration 5
Rhythm: Rock

Words and Music by Doc Pomus
and Mort Shuman

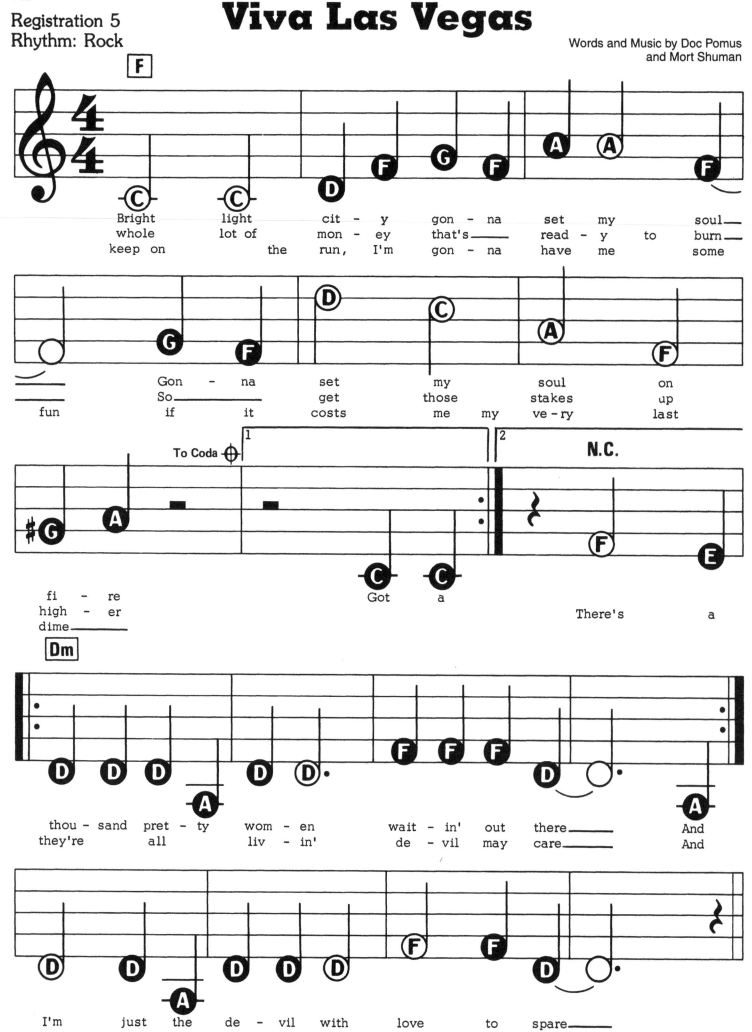

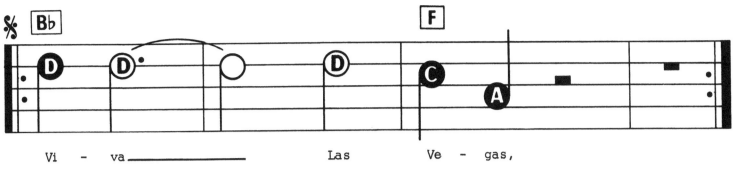

Vi – va_____ Las Ve – gas,

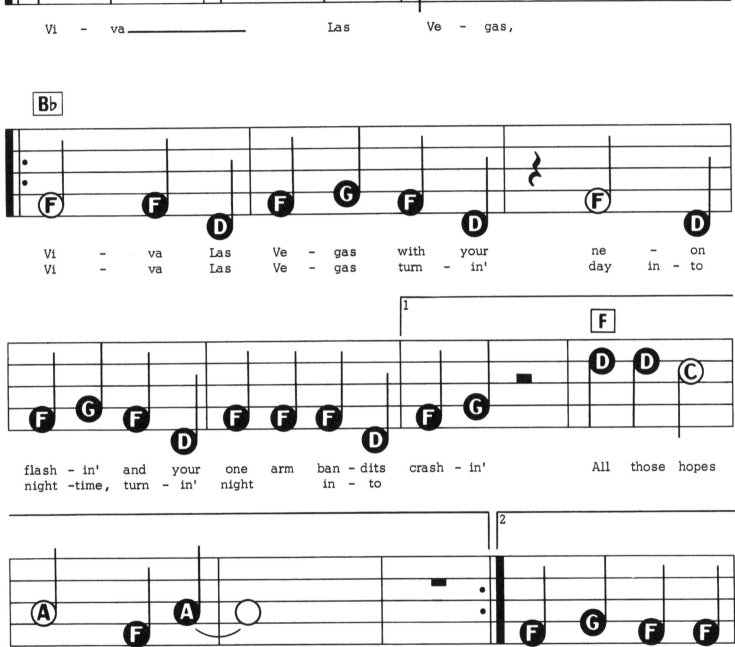

Vi – va Las Ve – gas with your ne – on
Vi – va Las Ve – gas turn – in' day in – to

flash – in' and your one arm ban – dits crash – in' All those hopes
night –time, turn – in' night in – to

down the drain_____ day – time, If you

see it once_____ you'll nev – er be the same_____ a – gain._____

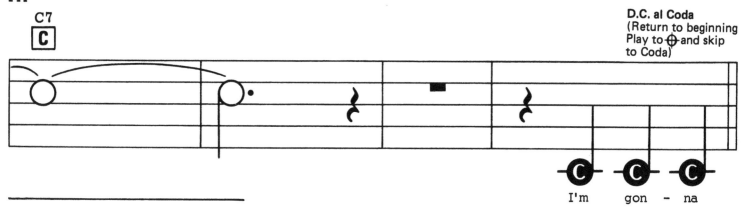

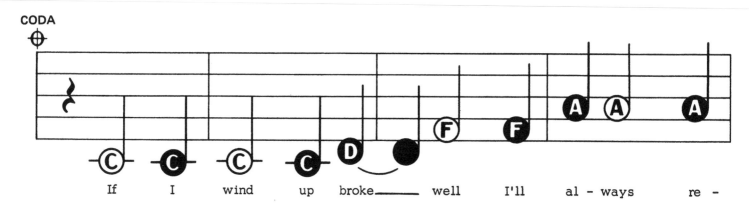

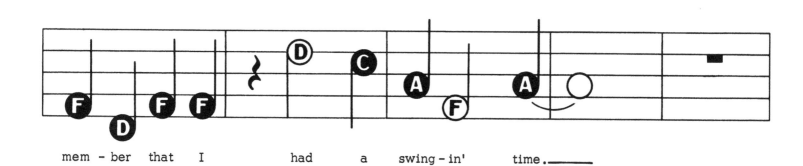

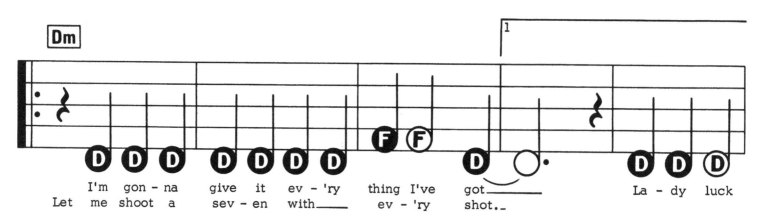

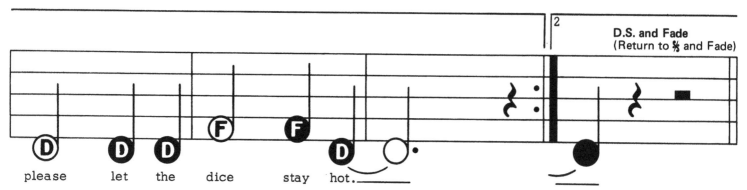

You Keep Me Hangin' On

Registration 5
Rhythm: Rock or 8 - Beat

Words and Music by Edward Holland,
Lamont Dozier and Brian Holland

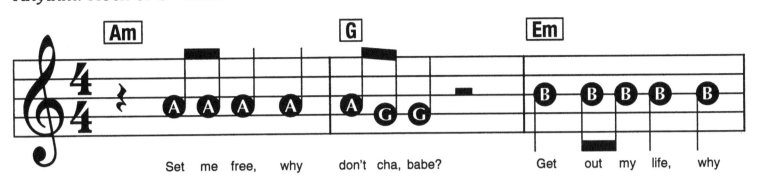

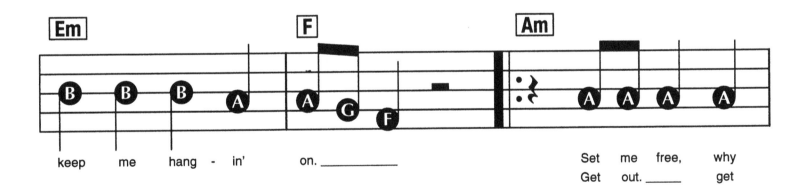

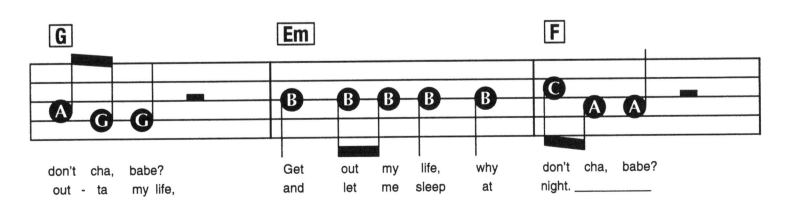

146

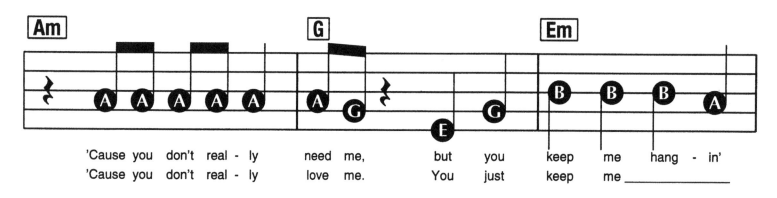

'Cause you don't real - ly need me, but you keep me hang - in'
'Cause you don't real - ly love me. You just keep me _____

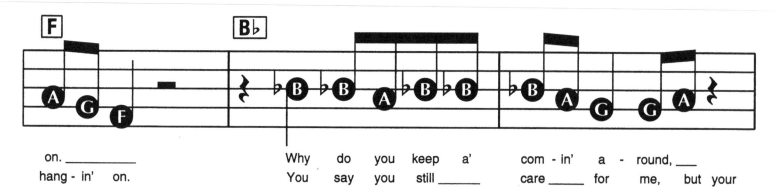

on. _____
hang - in' on.

Why do you keep a' com - in' a - round, ___
You say you still _____ care _____ for me, but your

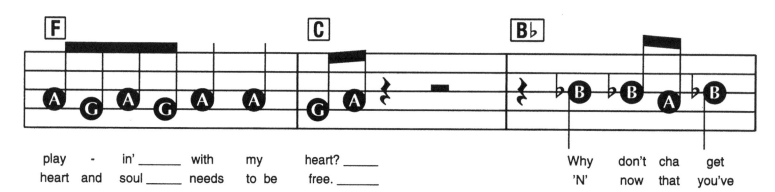

play - in' _____ with my heart? _____
heart and soul ____ needs to be free. _____

Why don't cha get
'N' now that you've

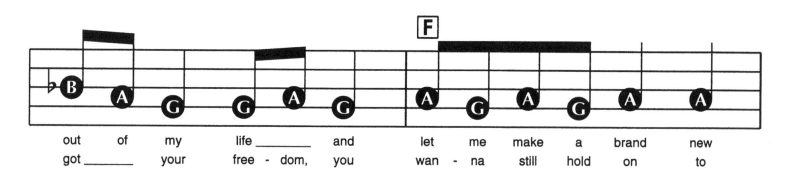

out of my life _____ and let me make a brand new
got _____ your free - dom, you wan - na still hold on to

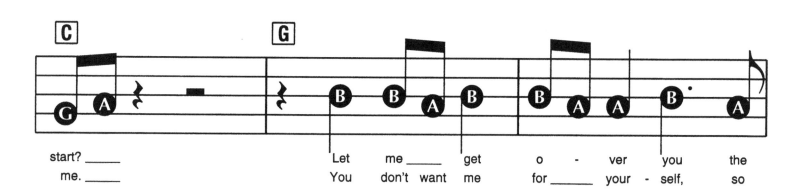

start? _____ Let me _____ get o - ver you the
me. _____ You don't want me for _____ your - self, so

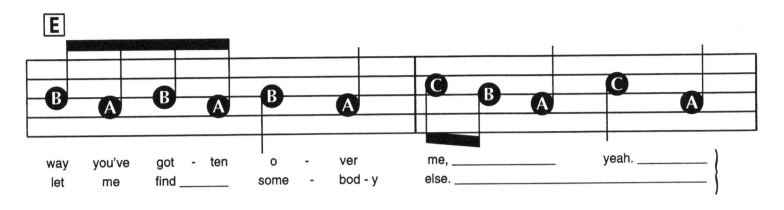

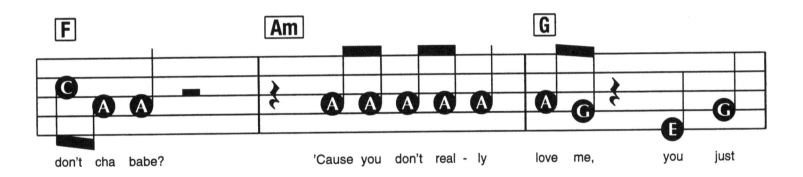

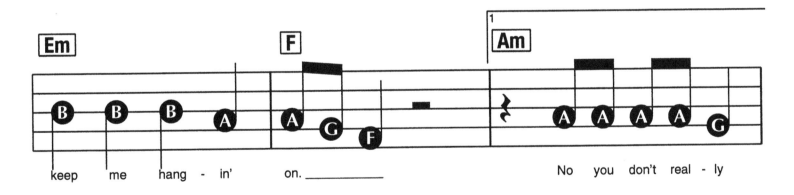

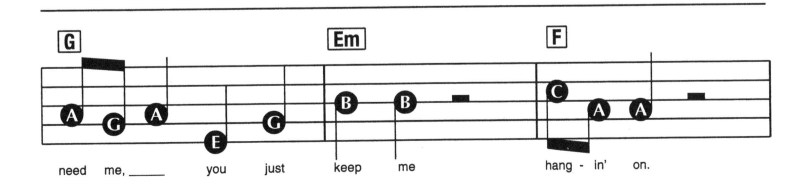

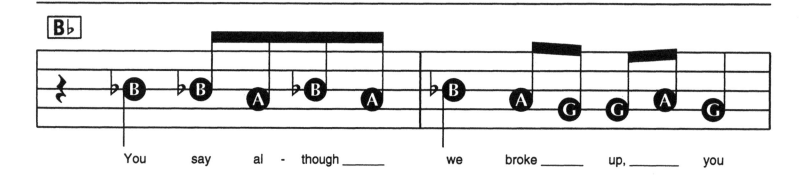

You say al - though _____ we broke _____ up, _____ you

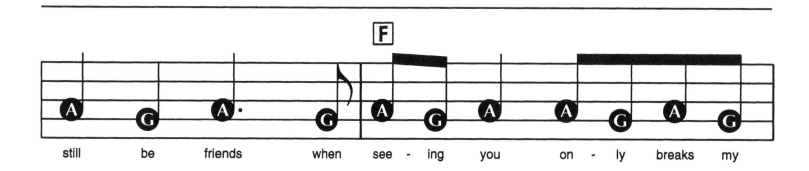

still just wan - na be friends. ___ But how can we

still be friends when see - ing you on - ly breaks my

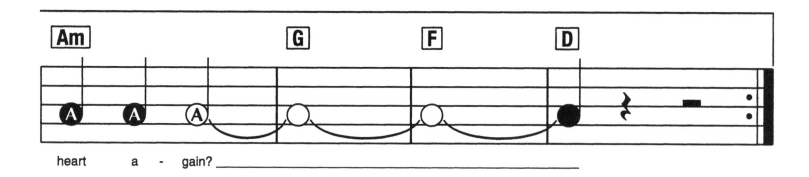

heart a - gain? _____

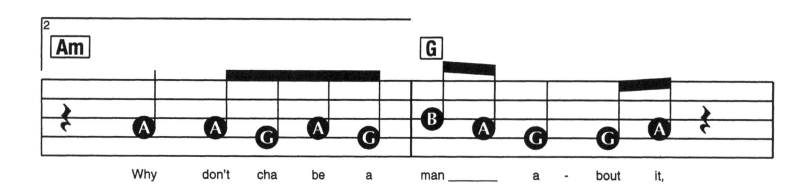

Why don't cha be a man _____ a - bout it,

149

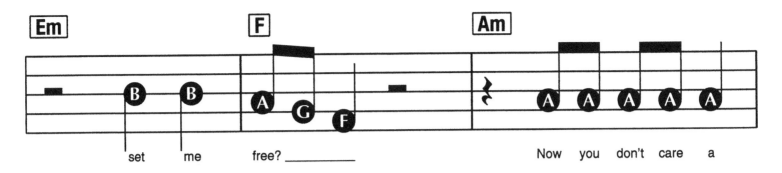

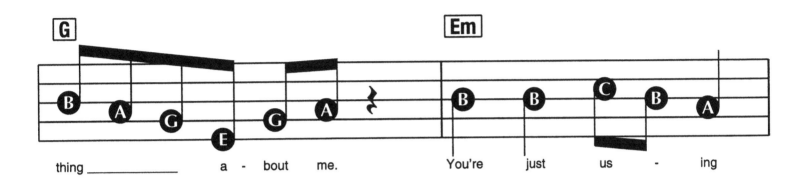

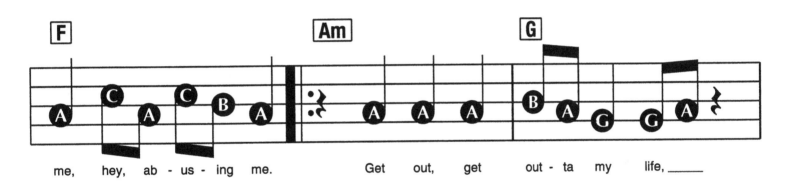

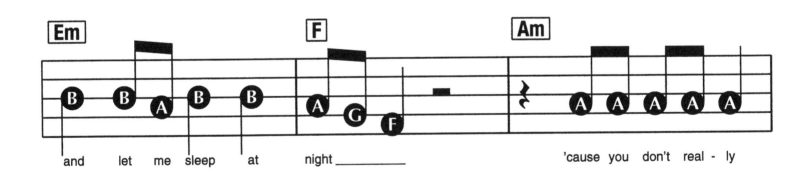

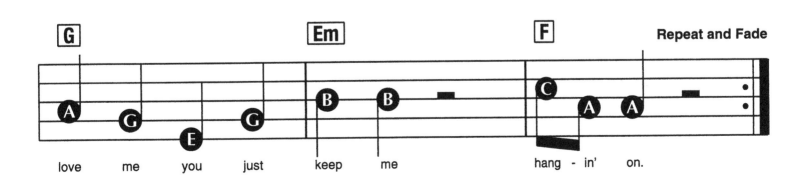

Wedding Bell Blues

Registration 4
Rhythm: Swing

Words and Music by
Laura Nyro

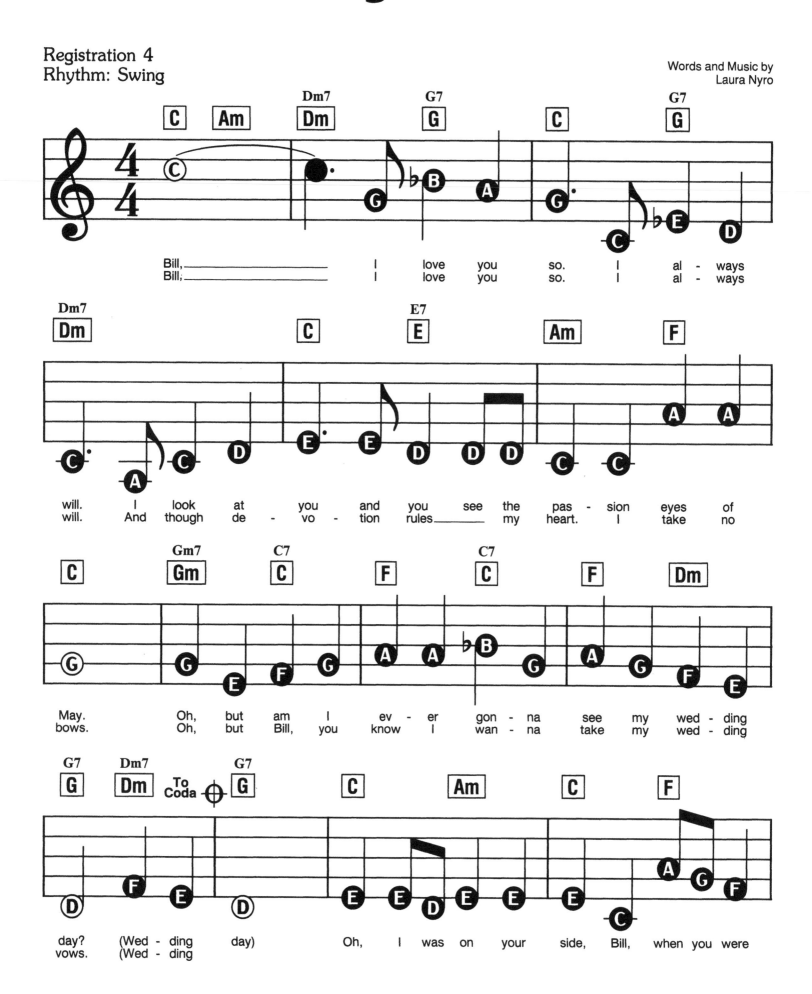

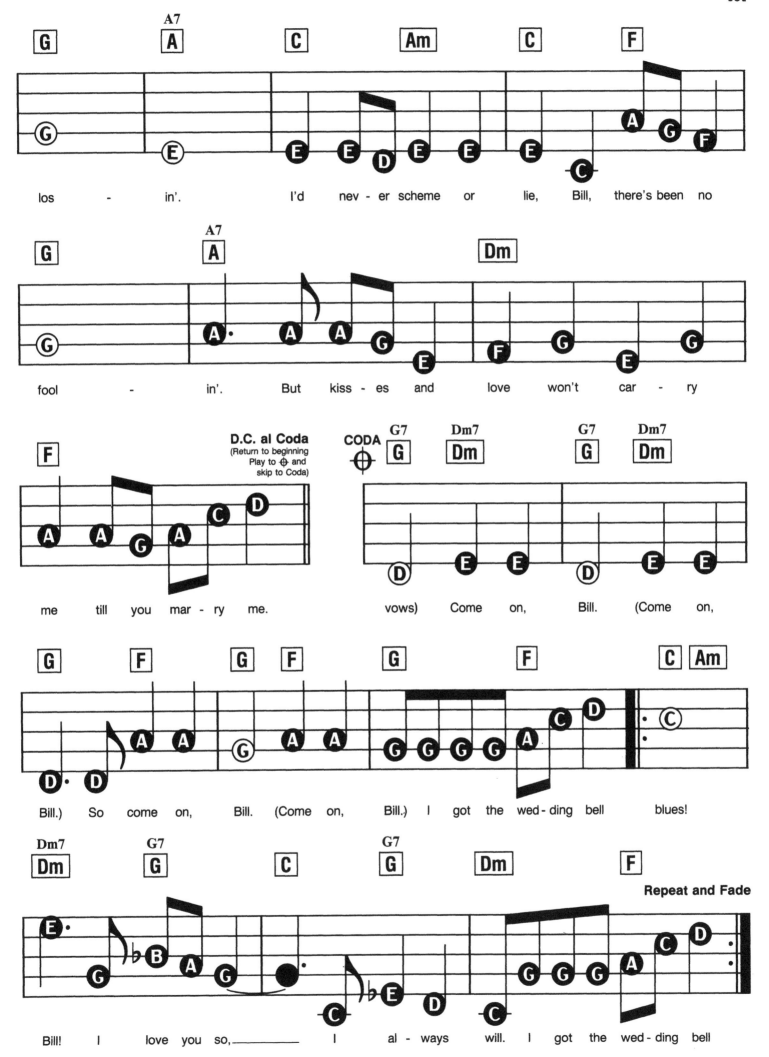

What Now My Love

Registration 2
Rhythm: Swing

Original French Lyric by Pierre Delanoe
Music by Gilbert Becaud
English Adaptation by Carl Sigman

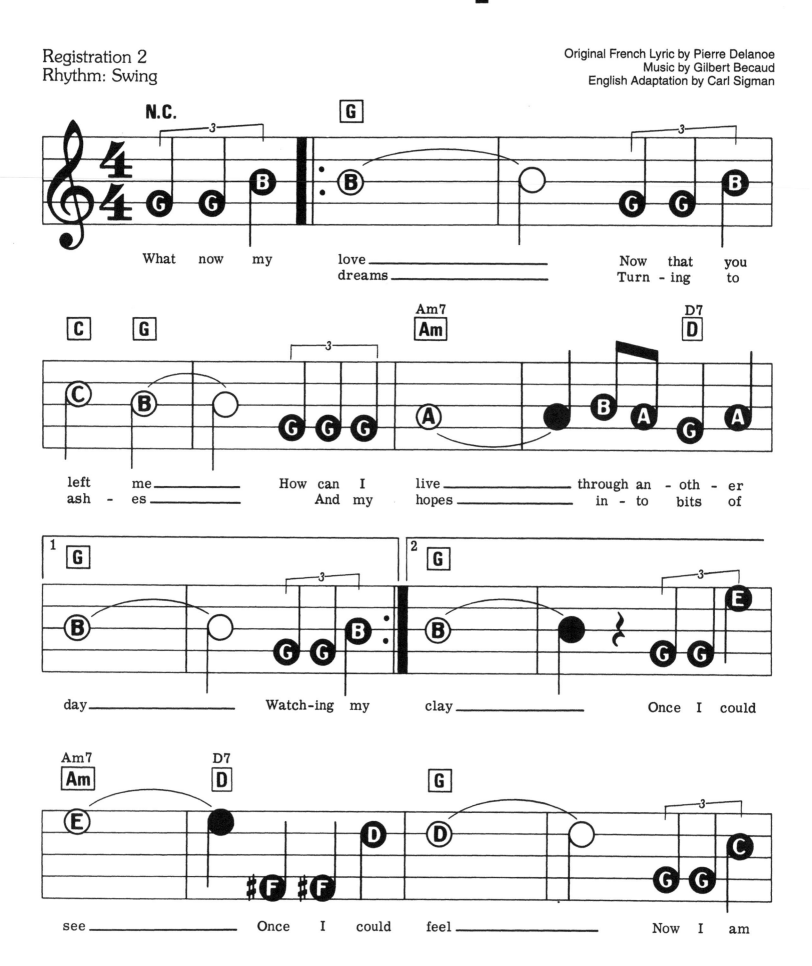

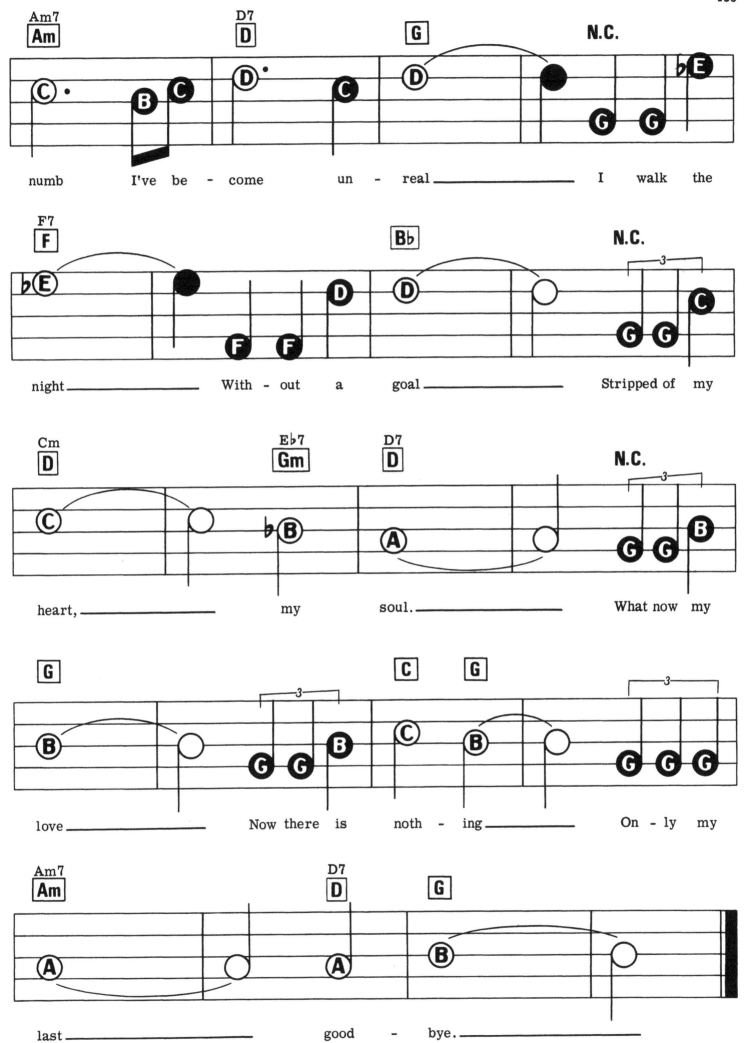

You've Lost That Lovin' Feelin'

Registration 1
Rhythm: Ballad or Slow Rock

Words and Music by Barry Mann,
Cynthia Weil and Phil Spector

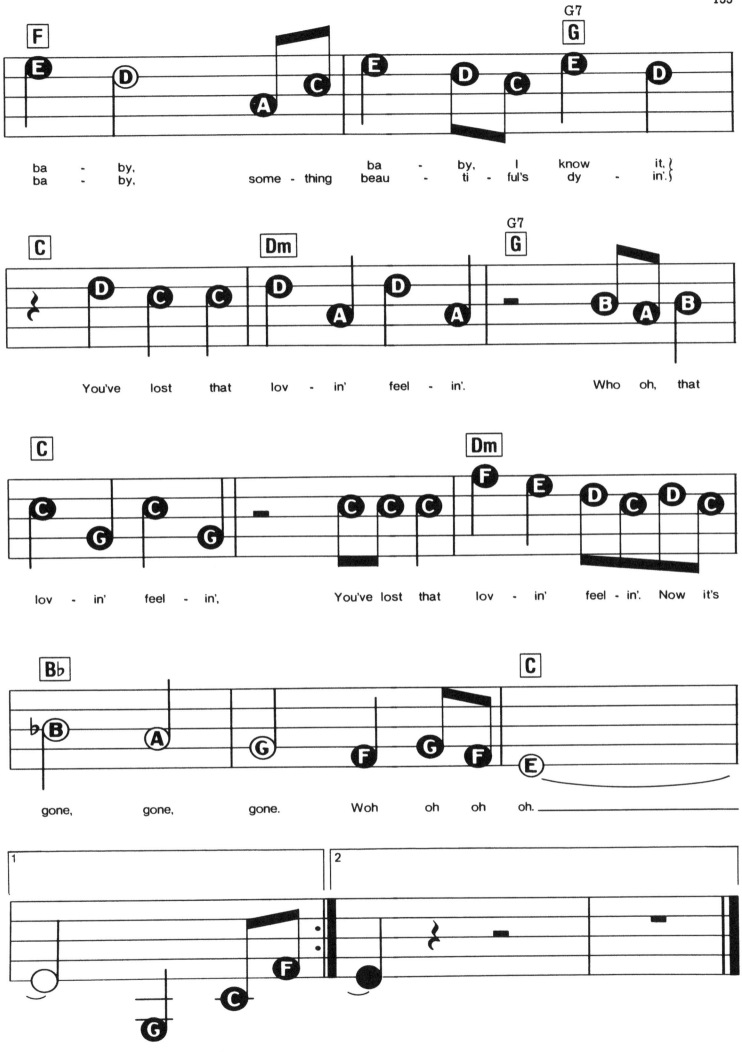

You've Made Me So Very Happy

Registration 1
Rhythm: Rock or 8 Beat

Words and Music by Berry Gordy, Frank Wilson,
Brenda Holloway and Patrice Holloway

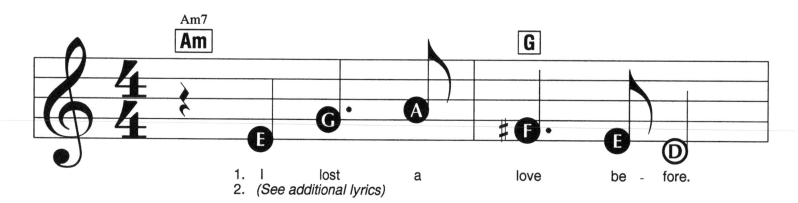

1. I   lost   a   love   be - fore.
2. *(See additional lyrics)*

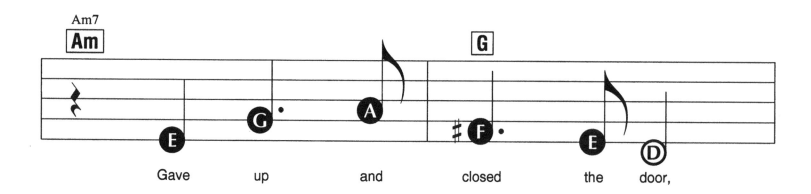

Gave   up   and   closed   the   door,

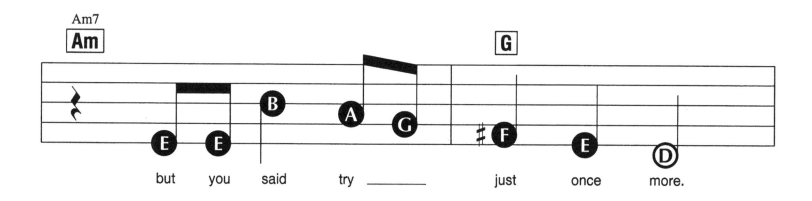

but   you   said   try _____   just   once   more.

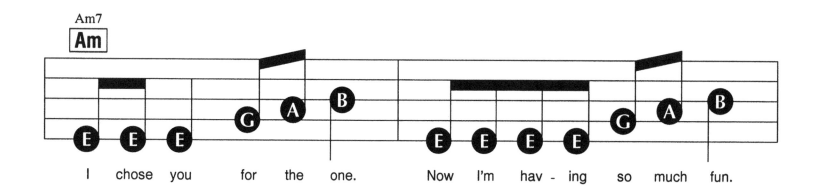

I   chose   you   for   the   one.   Now   I'm   hav - ing   so   much   fun.

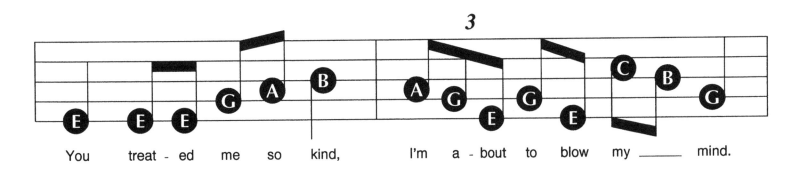

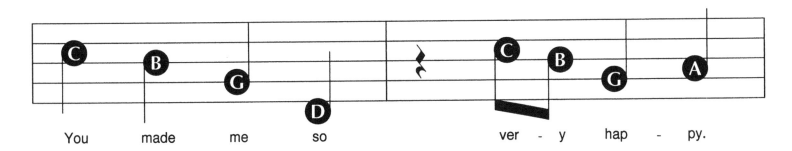

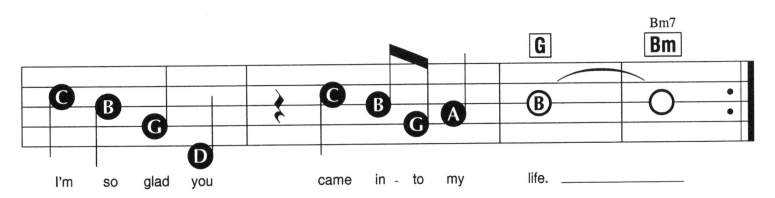

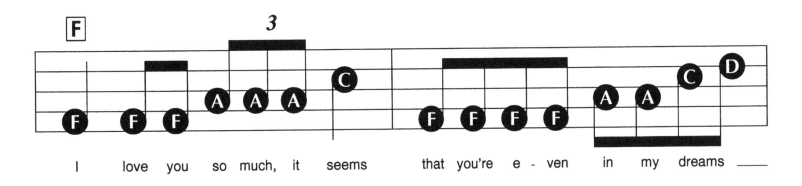

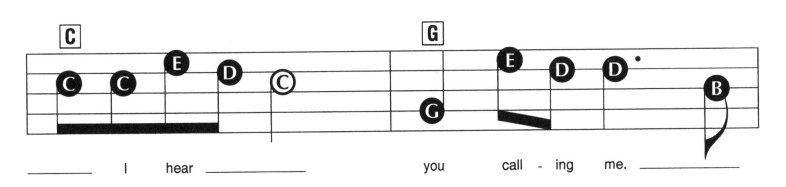

158

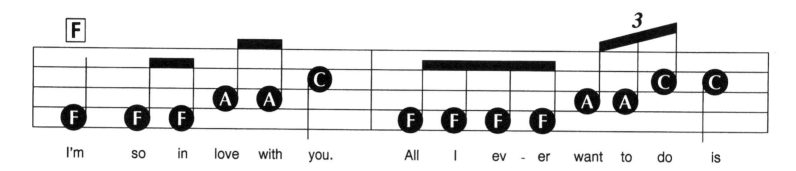

I'm so in love with you. All I ev - er want to do is

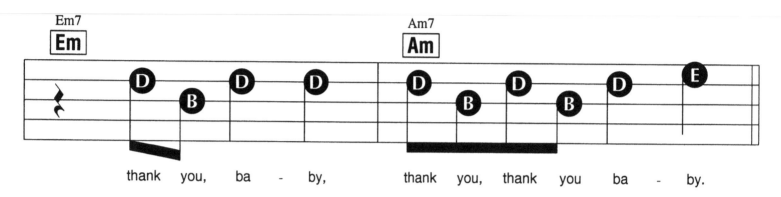

thank you, ba - by, thank you, thank you ba - by.

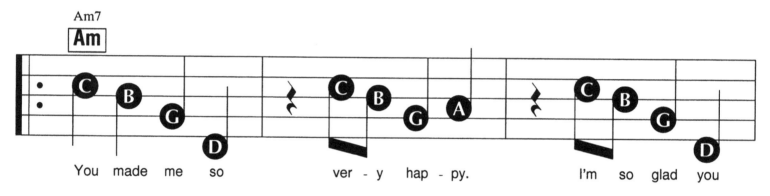

You made me so ver - y hap - py. I'm so glad you

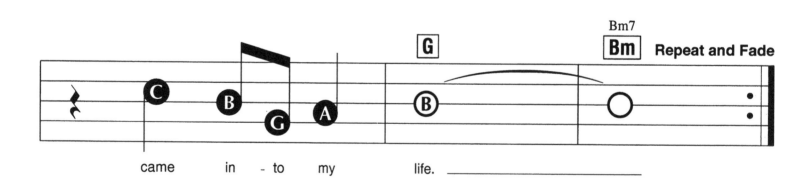

Repeat and Fade

came in - to my life. _____

Additional Lyrics

2. The others were untrue, but when it came to you,
   I'd spend my whole life with you.
   'Cause you came and took control,
   You touched my very soul.
   You always showed me that loving you was where it's at.

Registration Guide

- Match the Registration number on the song to the corresponding numbered category below. Select and activate an instrumental sound available on your instrument.

- Choose an automatic rhythm appropriate to the mood and style of the song. (Consult your Owner's Guide for proper operation of automatic rhythm features.)

- Adjust the tempo and volume controls to comfortable settings.

Registration

1	Flute, Pan Flute, Jazz Flute
2	Clarinet, Organ
3	Violin, Strings
4	Brass, Trumpet
5	Synth Ensemble, Accordion, Brass
6	Pipe Organ, Harpsichord
7	Jazz Organ, Vibraphone, Vibes, Electric Piano, Jazz Guitar
8	Piano, Electric Piano
9	Trumpet, Trombone, Clarinet, Saxophone, Oboe
10	Violin, Cello, Strings